# Serial Number Based Dating Guides for Vintage Ludwig Drums

# Main Line Drums 1963-1984 & Standard Drums 1968-1973

## by Richard E. Gier

## *Second Edition*

©2023 by Richard E. Gier

ISBN 978-1-888408-60-7

Rebeats Publications
P/O/ Box 6
Alma, Michigan 48801
www.rebeats.com

**COPYRIGHT INFRINGEMENT NOTICE**
The first edition of this book suffered frequent infringement. The preparation of this information involved thousands of hours of hard work. The author retains all rights, including the right to reproduce, distribute, display, and sell this work and to create derivative works based upon this work. You cannot scan or take a picture of an important table or graph and post it on an internet site; that violates the author's intellectual property rights. This is not excused by fair use exceptions to U.S. Trademark law. It also does not matter that you did not make any money from that act- what matters is the impact on potential sales of this publication. **Please honor the author's creative rights!**

# REVISED AND EXPANDED EDITION
## Serial Number-Based Dating Guides for Vintage Ludwig[1] Drums
## Main Line Drums 1963-1984 & Standard Drums 1968-1973

© Richard E. Gier 2013, 2023 All Rights Reserved

*In the ten years since my serial number-based dating guides for Ludwig drums were first published in 2013, the number of drums documented has nearly tripled. Using this largest known list of vintage Ludwig drums allows for refinement of prior observations and presentation of new observations which will help to date and authenticate vintage Ludwig drums.*

After first falling in love with the sound and look of vintage Ludwig drums, many wish to learn how to estimate their age and verify their authenticity. While several resources are available to assist with this endeavor, they are incomplete, inaccurate and easy to misinterpret. The guides for the 1970s are particularly lacking and Standards are completely ignored. Frustration with the limitations of the published resources inspires a fresh and detailed look at how to date and authenticate Ludwig drums.

With this revision, this paper documents information gathered from more than 17,600 vintage Ludwig drums (up from 6,300 in the first edition). It presents dating guides for main line drums produced in 1963-1984 and second line Standard drums produced in 1968-1973. It explores many of the nuances which make Ludwig drums of the 1960s and 1970s so interesting and, at times, so very frustrating. It discusses significant changes in hardware and other physical characteristics and identifies serial numbers and dates associated with these changes. It debunks some oft-repeated myths that permeate published materials, internet resources and the minds of some "vintage drum experts." It focuses on what the drums reveal about themselves and provides some much needed clarity to the sometimes unclear world of vintage Ludwig drums.

Information is presented in six parts. Part I reviews the published serial number-based dating resources for Ludwig drums. Part II provides new serial number based dating guides for main line Ludwig drums bearing Keystone, Blue/Olive and Large Keystone badges produced from late 1963 through 1984. Part III explores many changes in physical characteristics of main line drums from 1963 through 1984. Part IV presents the only published serial number-based dating guide for Ludwig's second line Standard drums produced from 1968 through 1973 and also explores changes in physical characteristics for Standards. Part V discusses the mystery of Date Codes used during 1971-1972 on both main and second line drums. Part VI presents information about vintage Ludwig drums with badges without serial numbers.

### PART I – THE PUBLISHED SERIAL NUMBER-BASED DATING RESOURCES

Before 2013, a drum owner could select from six published dating resources when they wanted to estimate the manufacturing date of a vintage Ludwig drum which lacked an indication of the manufacture date on the drum. They are authored by (in chronological order): Paolo Sburlati, Clay Taylor Greene, Mike Machat, Ned Ingberman, Rob Cook and John Aldridge.[2] The authors present information in

---

[1] The author is not associated with Ludwig Drum Company, Ludwig Industries or Conn-Selmer Inc., the current owner of the Ludwig trademark.

[2] Paolo Sburlati, Ludwig: Yesterday and Today, Paolo Sburlati Enterprises, Turin, Italy, 1999; Clay Taylor Greene, originally posted at LudwigDrummer.com, now https://www.vintagedrumguide.com/serial_numbers.html. Greene's original effort dates to March 8, 2002; Mike Machat, "Serial Number and Date List for Vintage Ludwig Drums (1963-1972), A practical guide for drum restoration and for verifying the build date and originality of your

two ways, reporting known serial number and date stamp combinations or presenting numerical ranges to demonstrate the general relationship between serial numbers and date stamps. All six resources addressed main line Keystone badge drums of the 1960s and four venture into the Blue/Olive badges which followed. None of these resources address Ludwig's second line Standard drums produced in the 1968-1973 era. Most seeking quick guidance regarding the age of their drums encounter Greene, Ingberman or Cook's guides because they are readily available via internet searches.

When all six of the resources are shown together, some of their similarities and differences become apparent. Graph 1 shows individual serial number/date stamp pairs and serial number date ranges provided in the six published resources for Keystone badge and early Blue/Olive badge drums from 1963 through early 1972. Graph 2 contains the published information available from Sburlati, Machat, Greene and Cook for Blue/Olive badge drums from late 1969 through 1980.[3]

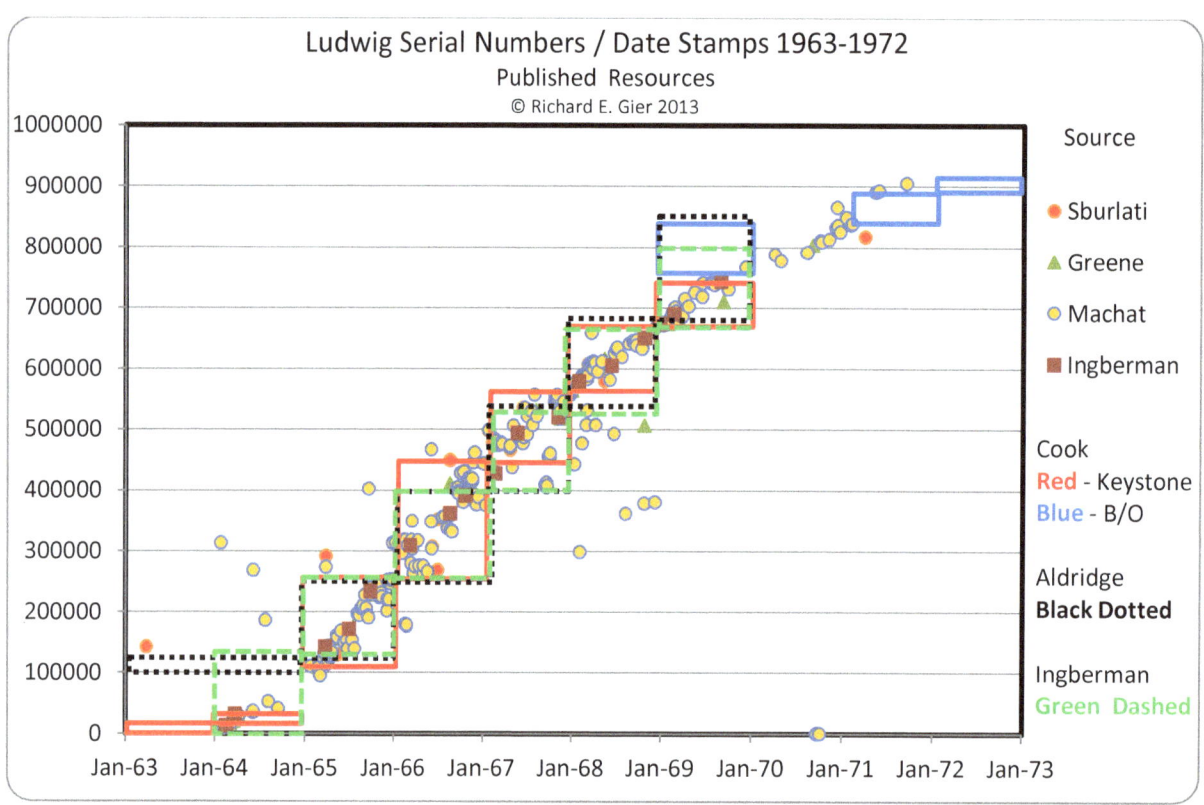

Graph 1 – Serial Numbers/Date Stamps for Keystone and Early Blue/Olive Badge Drums

---

vintage Ludwig drums," self-published, 2002; Ned Ingberman, "How To Date 1960's Ludwig Drums By Serial Numbers," DRUM! Magazine, Sep/Oct 2002, p. 126, with a modified version available at http://www.vintagedrumguide.com/ludwig_serials.html; Rob Cook, The Ludwig Book, Rebeats Publications, Alma, MI (2003), p. 210 (excerpt available at the Ludwig Drum Company website - https://www.ludwig-drums.com/en-us/ludwig/serial-guide, but with errors) Note that Cook recently revised The Ludwig Book to direct readers to the guide you are currently reading; John Aldridge, "Chaotic Creativity: Ludwig Drum Sets In The '60s," DRUM! Magazine, July 2005. Information from the six resources can be found in other guides, often without attribution.

[3] For Sburlati, only those with actual dates were used for Graph 1 while those with estimated dates were included in Graph 2. Greene presents only one data point for Blue/Olive badge drums not already provided by Sburlati.

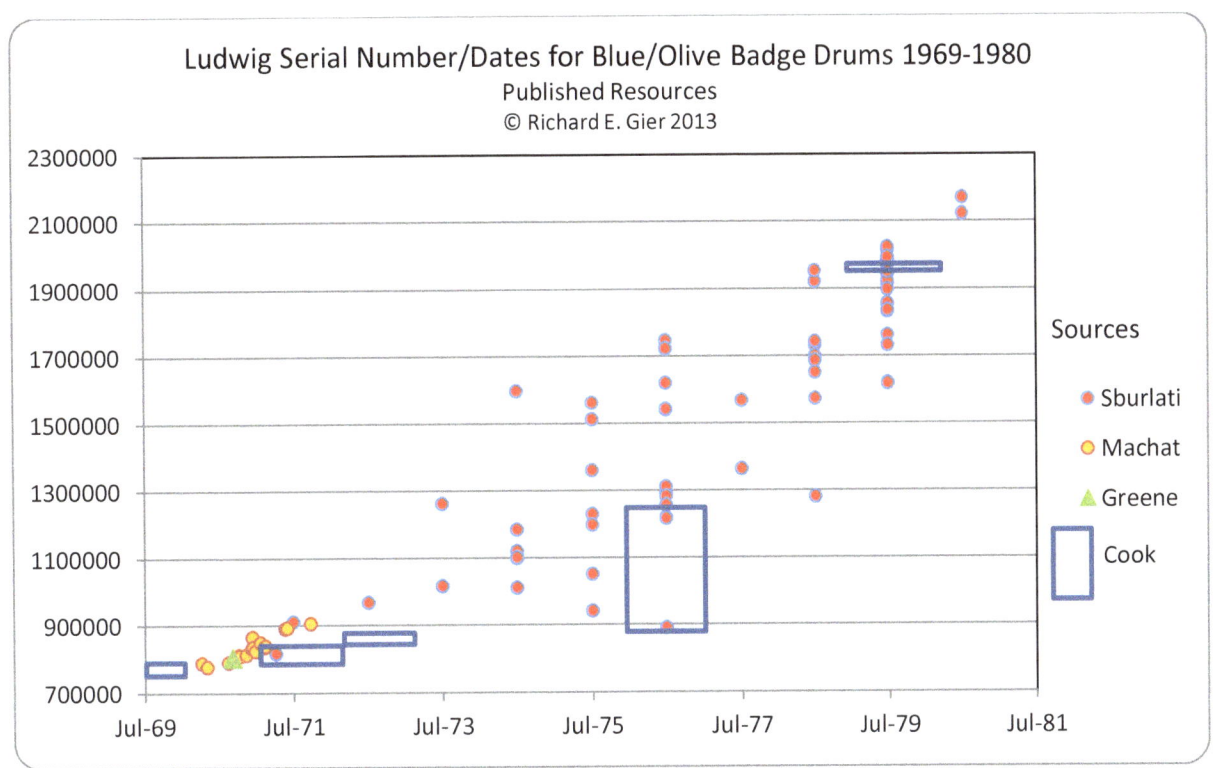

Graph 2 – Serial Numbers/Dates for Blue/Olive Badge Drums from Published Sources

All six resources provide reasonably consistent results for the 1960s Keystone badge era. They vary considerably for the Blue/Olive badge era. All six possess limitations which leave them susceptible to both innocent misunderstanding and opportunistic misinterpretation.

Limitation #1 - Not Enough Data. Most rely upon very few data points. Sburlati reports 44 drums with both serial numbers and date stamps, Greene lists 70 and Ingberman lists 17.[4] Readers of these three guides should be careful about drawing conclusions based upon small sample sizes. Fortunately, not all of the published guides suffered this limitation.[5] Cook relies upon more than 150 serial number/date stamp pairs to develop his annual ranges.[6] Machat contains information from 304 drums which have serial numbers and date stamps. Only four of the six resources address the Blue/Olive badge era, and none does much justice. Machat, with 18 drums, has the most reports of Blue/Olive badge drums with both serial numbers and date stamps. Sburlati reports 88 Blue/Olive badge drums, but only three of them have actual date stamps. The remaining drums possess estimated dates.

Limitation #2 - Duplicated Data. Many utilize the same underlying data. Greene includes 17 drums which appear in Sburlati's book. Thirty-six of Machat's drums appear in Sburlati or Greene, or both. The vast majority of Cook's data is from Sburlati and Machat.[7] In addition, Aldridge relies upon information from Cook and others.[8] While there is nothing inherently wrong about using some of the

---

[4] Ingberman reviewed "many, many hundreds" of drums to develop his guide, although because he lists only 17 drums hand selected to represent them, it is not immediately apparent from looking at just the charts that more drums were involved. Email exchange with Ned Ingberman, November 11, 2013.
[5] Aldridge does not indicate how many data points he used.
[6] Cook graciously shared his research file with the author.
[7] Cook combined an early list from Machat and emails from Sburlati and a few other collectors with his own data.
[8] Email exchange with John Aldridge, July 12, 2013.

same data points, it can be a situation akin to insufficient diversity in the gene pool. The use of the same underlying data has a predictable outcome - the results tend to mirror each other. In addition, errors in one resource are perpetuated when repeated in another.

<u>Limitation #3 - Erroneous Data.</u> They contain data which is known to be or is very likely to be erroneous. Close review of each resource reveals potential problems. Sburlati has a few instances where date stamps described in the text do not agree with the associated pictures. In one instance, two different date stamps are apparently attributed to the same drum on different pages of the book, although a careful reading reveals that the second date stamp belongs to a different drum. Also, most of Sburlati's 1970s dates appear to be estimates, although they are not always described as such. Most of the confusion stems from the layout of the information or from clarity issues, understandable because the text is written in Italian with an English translation.

Greene substitutes a January 1 date for 22 drums where only a year was known, skewing the data and misleading many. Most who encounter Greene's list are not aware that almost one-third of the dates are inaccurate because Greene's disclosure of this data manipulation on the ludwigdrummer.com website was lost when just the tables were extracted and the original site went dark. Further, Greene sometimes disagrees with information on drums shown in Sburlati's book.

Machat's raw data possesses a large number of outlying points. At least some of these points appear to be the result of inaccurate reports or record keeping errors and do not reflect actual variations in the Ludwig production process. In fairness, Machat did not anticipate that his informal list originally intended for his personal use would be used as part of a broader and more detailed study and acknowledges that it may contain data recording errors.[9] One error in Machat's data can be traced to Sburlati's apparent report of two different dates for the same drum. The questions surrounding Sburlati and Machat's data also taint Cook, as the majority of the data supporting Cook's ranges came from Machat with most of the remainder supplied by Sburlati.

Errors in data collection are very understandable. While collecting data for this project, the author encountered many difficult to read stamps and many online listings where date stamps are misread or misreported. In particular, years 1965 and 1966, 1966 and 1968, or 1968 and 1969 often are misread and interchanged.[10] Manufacture dates of drums without date stamps are often declared by reference to a drum's serial number alone, with an estimate obtained from one of the published resources. In addition, when unsure of a year in a blurred date stamp, many estimate the date based upon the serial number and then declare what the date stamp likely says. Such self-fulfilling prophesies do not result in objectively reliable data, they just perpetuate the confusion. Further, Date Codes, which are explored in Part V, are often misinterpreted as specific dates. Finally, switched badges and faked date stamps are also encountered but may be difficult to discern at the time of data collection. The author disregards date claims in cases where a clear determination can not be made, but cannot guarantee that a few errors did not slip through. It is not clear what level of scrutiny data gathered by multiple persons in multiple efforts received. Although data collected by others is not inherently untrustworthy, it is difficult for the author

---

[9] Email exchange with Mike Machat, June 19, 2013.
[10] An owner may describe a drum as from one year, while close review of pictures of a date stamp may reveal that it is from a different year. Note that misreading of date stamps can work both ways, making outlying points out of more ordinary drums or falsely representing ordinary drums as outliers. For example, consider a drum with a serial number that most would link to 1966. If the date says 1966 but is misread as 1968, an ordinary drum becomes an outlier. Conversely, if that drum's stamp is actually from 1968, but incorrectly recorded as from 1966, an outlier becomes ordinary.

to have complete confidence in the accuracy of the data used in the published guides given the multiple potential sources of error encountered during recent data collection efforts. Unfortunately it is too late to go back to verify the information collected years ago to create the published guides.

<u>Limitation #4 – Confusing/Misleading Presentation.</u> Their presentation of information is sometimes confusing and susceptible to misinterpretation. Much of the problem is the result of viewing the estimating tables apart from their accompanying explanations. Many users are tempted to quickly read a number off a table without understanding the origin of the information. This might work if the tables were more alike or easier to understand, but with the published resources, the results are inconsistent. Ingberman's Chart #1 shows dates and serial numbers which are all in neat order. As the dates advance, the serial numbers also follow in a remarkably uniform sequence. If one reads Ingberman's article, it is clear that he hand picks 17 drums to demonstrate the general relationship between date and serial number and cautions that drums could vary several months from the dates indicated in his charts. However, few appear to read and heed this warning. Many interpolate between points on Ingberman's Chart #1 and declare a specific month and year of manufacture despite the absence of a date stamp. This practice is misguided and produces estimates which, although more precise, are not any more accurate. In addition, Ingberman's Chart #2 provides ranges which reflect a constant annual production rate through the 1960s, which is an oversimplification considering information available now. Further, the annual ranges present specific start and stop points. Ingberman cautions that the endpoints are merely close indicators, but again, few listen. When viewed in isolation, Ingberman's charts fail to convey the considerable variability known to exist with Ludwig drums. Despite their shortcomings, because they are prominently displayed online, Ingberman's charts often serve as the beginning and end for many seeking quick answers. Those who believe that Ingberman's charts provide definitive answers are misinformed.

Greene's list of date stamps and serial numbers is grittier and shows more variability than Ingberman's. Some serial number/date stamp pairs look out of order, which is a better representation of the reality of 1960s Ludwig drums. However, Greene substituted "January 1" for 22 of his entries where only the year was known, making the data appear even more random than it actually is. Further, because Greene's table does not jive well with Ingberman's, less knowledgeable readers are often confused. Attempts to interpolate between points on Greene's chart generally fail because the data is not neat and orderly. This inability to obtain a more precise estimate with Greene's chart frustrates many and sends them back to misinterpret Ingberman's information. Others somehow find a way to erroneously use Greene's list to produce dates which are down-to-the-month precise.

Cook's table of annual serial number ranges achieves anointed status to many because it appears on Ludwig's website, albeit with one major alteration. Rather than rounding or estimating, Cook uses serial numbers from actual reported date stamped drums to represent the endpoints for each year. While an improvement over Ingberman's Chart #2, Cook's table also has some shortcomings. Several serial number ranges are skipped, leaving gaps of tens of thousands of neglected drums. Also, Cook's ranges do not indicate any overlap of serial numbers from year to year, leading many to incorrectly treat the endpoints of his ranges as precise and absolute when they are only representative examples. Like Ingberman's Chart #2, this is a limitation of all guides which present annual ranges with discrete endpoints where the fuzziness of the endpoints is not clearly expressed or appreciated.

As the only of the three more popular guides which ventures into the 1970s, Cook's 2003 chart becomes the authoritative resource on the subject of dating of Blue/Olive badge drums. However, Cook shows several years (1973-1975 and 1977-1978) where no drums are reported and one year (1976) where seemingly too many are reported. As a result, many with Blue/Olive badge drums who take Cook's table at face value conclude that their drums were made in 1976. Further, many reach incorrect conclusions because not all badges from 1970 are unnumbered or out of sequence as Cook's table indicates. Although Cook explains his chart in the accompanying text in his book, many have only seen the chart and do not appreciate the totality of the situation. As with the Keystone-era portion of his guide, the precision of the endpoints of the annual ranges are often given too much credit. While Cook's willingness to address the 1970s is appreciated, his presentation makes the 1970s drums appear to be much more haphazard than they are. Nonetheless, up until 2013, Cook provided the most complete published information available for this era.[11]

As of the date of publication of this revised guide, Ludwig's website displays a dating chart based upon Cook's chart from the 2003 edition of <u>The Ludwig Book</u>, but Ludwig incorrectly repeats the serial numbers used in 1967 and 1968 as if they were also used in the years 1978 and 1979. Many who rely upon their two minutes of internet research to date their drums find this misinformation on Ludwig's own website and are left convinced that it actually happened that way. Spoiler Alert – IT DIDN'T.

Machat's list contains 304 serial number/date stamp pairs, grouped by year with an indication of where serial numbers seemed to overlap between years. It does the best job of presenting the frequency and magnitude of the variations in the serial number/date stamp relationship. Unfortunately, this early work is not well known and is difficult to find. For those who can find it, Machat's raw data permits improved understanding of the basis of Cook's chart. It also highlights the amount of variation in the serial number/date stamp relationship in a very difficult to ignore manner. For those who like to see the numbers, it offers by far the most detail of the published resources. While Machat's work lives on by virtue of Cook's use of an earlier version of his list, Cook presents summaries instead of listing raw data, so the impact is blunted. Finally, Machat offers little analysis beyond identifying drums which have serial numbers which seem lower or higher than expected given their date stamps, leaving opportunity for wide speculation about the meaning of his data.

> **MYTH – Most Blue/Olive Badge drums were manufactured in 1976.**
> **TRUTH – The guides greatly exaggerate the serial number range of drums manufactured in 1976.**

One particular drum set from Sburlati appears to greatly impact the published guides.[12] The drums at issue are a red, silver and blue sparkle set with serial numbers in the 89XXXX range shown on page 42 of Sburlati's book. Sburlati identifies these drums as from 1976 due to the timing of the American bicentenial and the set's patriotic colors, but does not provide any further rationale for the 1976 date. Meanwhile, Machat reports a drum with a February 1972 date stamp with a serial number in the 916XXX range and several others from 1971 and 1972 with serial numbers above 900000. Cook attempts to reconcile the two sources, setting 916XXX as the high serial number for 1972 and 917XXX as the lowest serial number in his broad range for 1976 in order to *almost* include the Sburlati "bicentenial set." However, Sburlati's set is more likely from 1971 or 1972. If it is, then perhaps Cook need not contort so much to try to include this data and the vintage drum world can stop incorrectly labeling such a large number of Blue/Olive badge drums as being from 1976. To further complicate matters, deeper research determines that Machat's February 1972 drum setting the bottom end of the range is actually a drum with Date Code 21720, which may not represent a February 1972 date at all. Unfortunately, Sburlati's

---

[11] It is clear from review of Cook's serial number research file that he attempted to find the best fit based upon the sometimes sparse and somewhat conflicting information available to him.

[12] Gier, Richard E., "How America's Bicentennial Impacted Ludwig Drum Dating" September 30, 2020. Available at http://www.gretschdrumdatingguide.com/other-projects.html, and in September 30, 2020 issue of Not So Modern Drummer.

misidentified Bicentennial drum set finds its way to Ludwig's website, which perpetuates these errors by continuing to use Cook's flawed 2003 chart and then adds errors of its own, discussed above.

<u>Limitation #5 – Misreading and Misuse.</u> Many people misread and misuse them. Like any tool, the serial number-based dating guides can be used to enlighten or to obfuscate. The majority looking at these guides are not vintage drum experts, just people who want to know their drum's age. Most interpret the guides without understanding their limitations and end up with faulty estimates. Others are drum collectors who see the guides as if chiseled in stone, find definitive answers where they do not exist and declare that a particular drum was manufactured in a particular month and year. Instead of acknowledging that they are dealing with an inexact science, they often defend their conclusions with a hearty "because the date guides say so!" This group of misinformed souls then propagates when they pass on their "wisdom and knowledge" to others who know even less than they do about vintage drums. This issue is especially rampant in Facebook Groups dedicated to vintage Ludwig drums. The problem could also be the careless use of imprecise language which overstates the accuracy of date estimates. More often it is an attempt to make someone appear more knowledgeable or a drum more valuable.

One final group of less than scrupulous individuals exploit the lack of clear and definitive information by glossing over inconsistencies in non-original drums they assemble from disparate parts. They then ask inflated prices for their instruments, often making false claims about their drums' originality to mislead potential buyers. The same few people seem to be the ones selling the majority of the drums that do not fit the general patterns. These individuals, who have superior knowledge of vintage drums and ready access to spare parts, are often the ones who remain suspiciously silent about their drums' histories, disclaim any expertise about drums or make loud but unsupported claims about the purity of their offerings. There should be a special ring in drum hell for these folks.

> **MYTH** – The manufacture date of a Ludwig drum can be accurately determined to within one month based solely upon its serial number.
> **TRUTH** – Accurate estimates which are precise to the month are not currently possible.

The actual practice of dating of Ludwig drums is interesting to observe. When a drum has a serial number and date stamp that fit in the general pattern predicted by the guides, it is accepted as authentic barring any obvious manipulation and modifications. If a drum has no date stamp, a date estimate is determined by reference to the guides discussed above and other physical characteristics are examined to determine if they are consistent with that date estimate. While the precision of such an estimate is often overstated, a knowledgeable person can make a reasonable determination of a drum's age and authenticity in this manner.

Meanwhile, when drum a possesses a serial number/date stamp combination that does not fit the guides or displays other characteristics inconsistent with its serial number or date stamp, the guides are often conveniently ignored and the drum is heralded as a prototype, "transition drum" or just another example of how Ludwig never wasted anything. The explanation for a deviant drum is often: "the shell must have been at the back of the shelf" or "the badge must have been at the bottom of the bin." These two reasons were presented by Sburlati in 1999 and have been repeated frequently ever since. It seems just as likely that such drums are altered in some way, the date stamps or serial numbers are misread, or the date stamps or badges are not original to the drum. With all of this uncertainty, it is possible for the less scrupulous to assemble drums from parts which did not leave the factory together and pass then off as all original drums despite their unusual combination of features.

This selective interpretation is further exemplified in the case of factory original "born together" sets. When serial numbers or date stamps within a set are tightly grouped, this is touted as proof that the set came together from the factory, even though drums assembled on the same day may have serial numbers or date stamps which are quite far apart. Conversely, when serial numbers or date stamps in a set cover a broader range, it is argued that they still came together from the factory because serial numbers and date stamps are acknowledged to have been used out of order. A recent attempt to allow objective analysis of these claims, a study of 437 allegedly "born-together" sets, concludes that some original "born-together" sets exhibit a range of serial numbers of more than 30,000.[13]

**MYTH – A factory original born together set has consecutive or nearly consecutive serial numbers and identical or nearly identical date stamps on all drums. Any combination of drums that differ more than a few hundred in serial number or a few weeks in date was not sold together originally.**
**TRUTH – Due to production variations and a myriad of other factors, serial numbers and date stamps on reported factory born together sets may differ considerably from drum to drum within the set.**

It often seems that spinning information in ones' favor knows few bounds. When it comes time to describe a vintage Ludwig drum, it seems that any drum that fits the guides is really rare, valuable and factory original, and any drum that does not fit the guides is also really rare, valuable and factory original. Few seem to possess drums that are typical or ordinary, even though Ludwig produced hundreds of them every single day. Fewer still admit that their drums are an amalgamation of drum parts assembled together to make a profit or drums which were modified during their four to six decade lives.

The serial number-based dating guides published before 2013, despite their limitations, are very helpful. However, the limitations of the published guides and a general lack of understanding of those limitations leave the guides subject to misunderstanding and misuse. Cautions provided by the authors have been lost or are ignored during the frenzied search for answers. Vintage drum owners can best assess the authenticity of their drums if they understand the strengths and weaknesses of these guides and have improved tools and expanded information available to assist them in their efforts.

### PART II – TWO NEW DATING GUIDES FOR MAIN LINE LUDWIG DRUMS

Two new dating guides were presented and are now updated, one for the 1963-1972 era when drums were date stamped and one for the 1972-1984 era which followed. Because the data available to support these guides varied, different approaches were utilized to create each.

**A. Date Guide for Main Line Ludwig Drums Manufactured 1963-1972**

The author gathered information from 3,394 previously undocumented main line drums with date stamps - 3,289 which possess serial numbers and 105 without serial numbers.[14] In many cases, both serial numbers and date stamps were viewed in person or seen in pictures, but some entries rely solely upon

---

[13] Gier, Richard E., "Brief Study of Serial Number Spans of "Born Together" Vintage Ludwig Drum Sets," http://www.gretschdrumdatingguide.com/other-projects.html, February 1, 2018

[14] Information from a total of drums 16,258 (15,243 gathered by the author and 1,015 contributed by others) is used to develop the dating guide for 1972-1984 presented in Part II.B. and to assist with analysis of changes in physical characteristics which are related to serial numbers and dates presented in Part III.

owner reports. Only drums possessing date stamps with discernible or reported months and years were used for the 1963-1972 dating guide.[15]

Information gathered includes: serial number, date stamp, ink color of date stamp, badge style, presence of interior paper label, drum type, drum dimensions, interior finish, tone control style, tone control felt color, hardware finish, type of strainer, number of lugs, style or model (i.e.: Clubdate, Jazz Festival, Acrolite), wrap or finish, sizes and serial numbers of accompanying drums if in a set, number of plies in the shell, the presence of rivets at the wrap seam and anything else of note. The categories of information sought expanded during the course of the study as additional aspects of Ludwig drums were identified and added. Information is collected from publically available internet resources, online auction listings, reports from vintage drum owners and physical inspection of available drums. Not all information is available for all drums, but whatever information is available is captured.

Much effort was taken to insure that the data used for this study was correctly read and recorded. Where a badge does not appear to be original to the drum, a date stamp does not appear to be authentic, or a serial number or date stamp cannot be determined with confidence, the information is not used. Drums from sellers who appear to engage in switching of badges, faking of date stamps and drum fabrication are also not used. Continuous review and vetting of the collected data is performed to minimize the presence of erroneous information. Despite the scrutiny applied to the data collection, this dating guide suffers from some of the same limitations as the published resources. Some of the data points may be incorrectly recorded or gathered from drums with undetected alterations. Importantly, this dating guide does not eliminate the variation within Ludwig's production process or magically attach badges with serial numbers in sequential order to shells stamped in date order. But, it does not gloss over the variations or make them easy to ignore. Armed with a much larger pool of data and a thorough understanding of how that data is collected and analyzed, the reader is better informed and able to use this guide with increased wisdom.

Graph 3 shows data collected by the author from 3,394 drums and demonstrates the strong relationship between serial numbers and date stamps between late 1963 and mid-1972. Variations occur, but the overwhelming majority of points are grouped closely around a gently sloping S-curve. Only about two percent of points have date stamps which are more than about six months or serial numbers which vary more than 50,000 in number from the general curve. Some of the outlying points represent variation resulting from Ludwig's production processes while some may be inaccurate information that managed to slip through the filters. It is urged that the reader focus upon the overwhelming number which conform to the general pattern and not on the relatively few which do not. When the drums without serial numbers are removed, one can use statistical analysis to model the relationship between serial number and date to produce a curve to fit the data. The calculated best-fit second degree polynomial trendline is then smoothed in the earliest days of serial numbers when production volume was considerably lower and in 1969-1971 when many drums were produced that did not receive serial numbers. The resulting trendline is then added to Graph 3.

---

[15] If the year and month are known or reported but the day is not, a drum is assumed to be from the first of the month. This impacts the integrity of the data somewhat, but not as much as applying a month and day when only the year was known as done by Greene. If anything less than both the month and year can be read or is reported, this data is not considered precise enough for use with Part II.A.

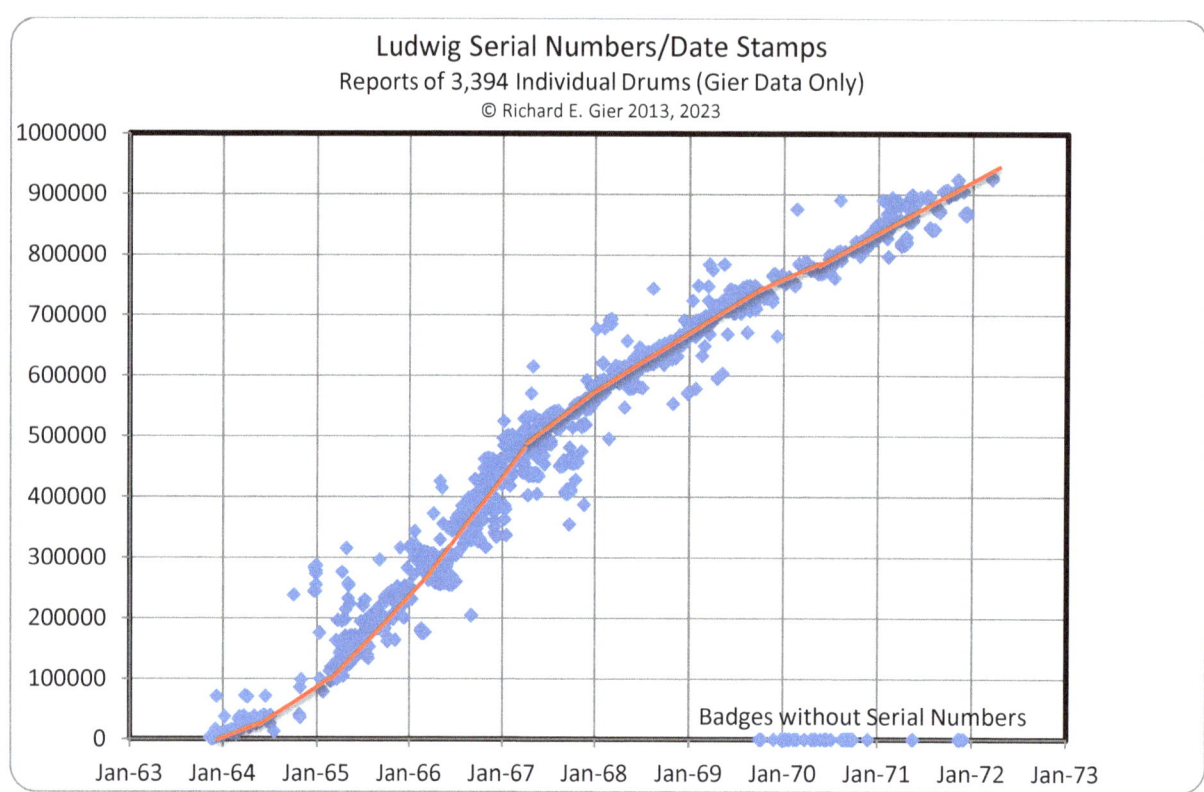

Graph 3 – Serial Numbers/Date Stamps - Gier Data Only

This study attempts to avoid or minimize the five limitations that affect the published guides. It relies upon far more data points than its predecessors. Each of those data points is independently gathered by the author. The data collection method is tightly controlled to limit the number of incorrectly read or reported date stamps and serial numbers. The information is presented in a manner which explains how the data was collected, providing details and summarizing information so that the reader can appreciate exactly how conclusions are reached. Hopefully fewer people will pass along faulty "wisdom" and fewer still will fall victim to those who prey on the uninformed.

This data suggests that Ludwig's date stamps and serial numbers are very highly correlated and not as varied as generally portrayed. The lament that "with Ludwig, anything could happen," appears to be highly overstated, at least where the serial number/date stamp relationship is concerned.[16] Anecdotes of boxes of overlooked badges and stacks of shells with unpopular finishes and sizes languishing on warehouse shelves for years create an incorrect impression that chaos ruled.[17] These stories often serve as the go-to explanations when drums do not seem to fit the expected patterns. However, many atypical drums are explained by careful reading of date stamps and serial numbers or realization that their badges have been altered or switched. While one must acknowledge that odd things happened from time to time, the overwhelming majority of Ludwig drums fall within the identified patterns. It appears that only

---

[16] Variations with hardware and other physical characteristics are explored in Part III of this paper.

[17] Drums produced with overlooked boxes of badges reintroduced into the badge supply would appear below the curve – lower serial numbers on shells with later date stamps. Drums produced using shells which were repeatedly passed over would appear above the curve – higher serial numbers on shells with earlier date stamps. The largest incidence of either phenomenon that is visibly apparent on Graph 3 is a cluster of drums with date stamps from July to December 1967 and serial numbers in the 400000 – 460000 range. These could be examples of the old badge/new shell variety. Note that insufficient data points are available to prove this explanation.

a relatively small number of Ludwig drums have factory original combinations of serial numbers and date stamps which vary significantly from expectations. These drums are fascinating topics for discussion and speculation precisely because they are so out of the ordinary. The existence of exceptions does not mean that there were no rules.

One can stop here and be content that a significant step is made in the dating of Ludwig drums. However, because many others share an interest in the topic, insight from other vintage drum enthusiasts is sought. Collector/historians Steve Black, the late Mike Layton and Mike Machat enthusiastically shared information they independently gathered for their own research purposes. Black focused on the late Keystone badge and early Blue/Olive badge drums and determining the transition point between them. Layton focused on correcting a repeated tendency to misidentify drums from 1965 as manufactured in 1964 and on determining when the baseball bat tone control is changed from red to white felt, so his entries are mainly from 1963-65. Machat, in addition to his earlier published effort, compiled a list of date stamped drums with six digit serial numbers on Blue/Olive Badges ("Machat II"). Black, Layton and Machat gathered information in different formats than the author, as none originally anticipated having their data used as part of this larger effort. While their data seems generally sound, verification and vetting of their data by the author is limited.

Combining data from Black, Layton, Machat and the author produces a second grouping of drums for evaluation. After eliminating duplications between contributors, the resulting database possesses a total of 3,865 drums - 3,722 with badges with serial numbers and date stamps and 143 with badges without serial numbers but with date stamps. Presented graphically in Graph 4, the relationship between serial number and date stamp is quite strong, even as variation is evident.

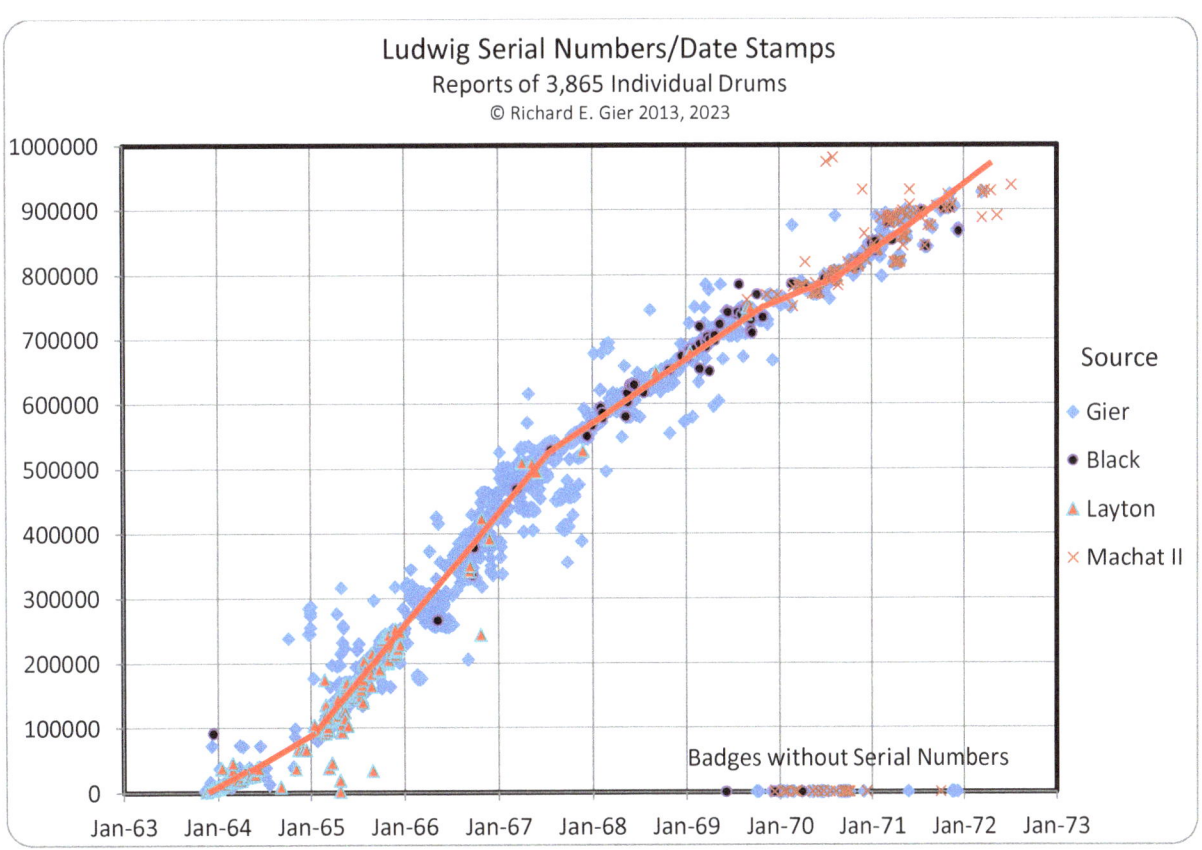

Graph 4 – Serial Numbers/Date Stamps from Gier/Black/Layton/Machat II

Removing the drums without serial numbers from this expanded group, statistical analysis and modeling is again performed. The resulting best-fit trendline is added on Graph 4, with the same smoothing adjustments made in Graph 3. Graphs 3 and 4 are very similar, although a slightly greater percent of points on Graph 4 are outliers. Even so, only about three percent of the data points in Graph 4 vary from the general curve by more than about six months in date or 50,000 in serial number. More data points do not eliminate the variation introduced by Ludwig's production processes. However, more data points allow us to increase our understanding of the variation.

Two sections of both Graph 3 and 4 appear to possess few data points. The first section is in the second half of 1964, with a corresponding serial number range of between about 40000 and 100000. Only nineteen drums with date stamps from July to December 1964 are recorded while 609 drums which lack date stamps are recorded from the 40000 - 100000 serial number range. These drums are fairly evenly distributed within that serial number range. Therefore, it does not appear that there are blocks of missing or skipped serial numbers to explain the lack of entries. It is possible that these drums never had date stamps or that this era of shells had stamps with ink that was particularly susceptible to being wiped off. There also do not appear to be any pre-serial number badges with date stamps from this time frame. Some might point out that the timing of the missing date stamps follows the first Beatles appearance on The Ed Sullivan Show and suggest that date stamps are missing because of the oft-reported surge in Ludwig's production volume. The data only shows that many drums in this serial number range exist, but very few of them have date stamps.

The second section is late 1969 to 1970. During this time period, a significant number of badges without serial numbers appear alongside badges with serial numbers. Because those without serial numbers appear along the X-axis of the graph and not on the curve with most of the other drums, they are easily overlooked. It is understandable why Cook's description for drums made in 1970 is "out of sequence, unnumbered" because unnumbered drums seem concentrated in this year, but this is an over-simplification. Four hundred and fifty-eight drums with 1970 date stamps are recorded; 337 of these have serial numbers and 121 do not.[18] Therefore, based upon these reports, about three-quarters of the 1970 drums do not appear to be any more "out of sequence" than the typical Ludwig serial number. If anything, they are closer to the trendlines and more tightly grouped than the typical data point. Only about one-quarter of the 1970 date stamped drums are unnumbered. A more in-depth discussion of Ludwig's use of badges without serial numbers is included in Part III.

It is suggested that either Graph 3 or 4 be used to approximate the date of a drum possessing a serial number in the following manner: find the serial number on the Y-axis, move horizontally until you reach the trendline, then follow that vertically down to the X-axis and determine the approximate date. Consider that as a mid-point for the approximate date of manufacture of the drum, and then add and subtract six months from this point to produce a reasonable estimate for a range for when the drum was made.

**Never state anything sounding remotely like, "Based upon Gier's graphs, the serial number on my drum indicates that it was made precisely on (insert specific date here)."** It is only an estimate. If one has a drum without a date stamp, they should simply recite the serial number and indicate that the date is estimated based upon that serial number. They should not attempt to state a date with a high

---

[18] These numbers may be overrepresented in the data collection because one is naturally drawn to the unusual incidents, and blank badges have received a lot of attention. It is suggested that a higher than average percentage of drums with blank badges are reported.

degree of certainty or precision because no date is stamped on the drum. At most one can say based upon this study is that a drum was **most likely** manufactured within a several month window.

To utilize all available information, data from all resources is combined onto one graph. The resulting Graph 5 combines the new Gier/Black/Layton/Machat II data with the published Sburlati/Greene/Machat I/Ingberman data. Unique data from the previously published works includes 44 reports from Sburlati, 31 from Greene,[19] 268 from Machat's 2002 list[20] and Ingberman's 17 handpicked examples. No information from Cook or Aldridge is included because they did not publish data from the individual drums. Graph 5 contains a total of 4,225 unique data points.

Graph 5 is very similar to Graphs 3 and 4 which used only newly gathered information, but contains considerably more outliers. Because of potential data irregularities and an inability to evaluate the data collection methods used by the authors of the published guides, this graph should not be used for date estimation purposes. This graph is shown to permit the reader to compare the published guides with the newly collected data. It should be reassuring to those who for years have relied upon the published guides that the stories depicted in these graphs are very similar.

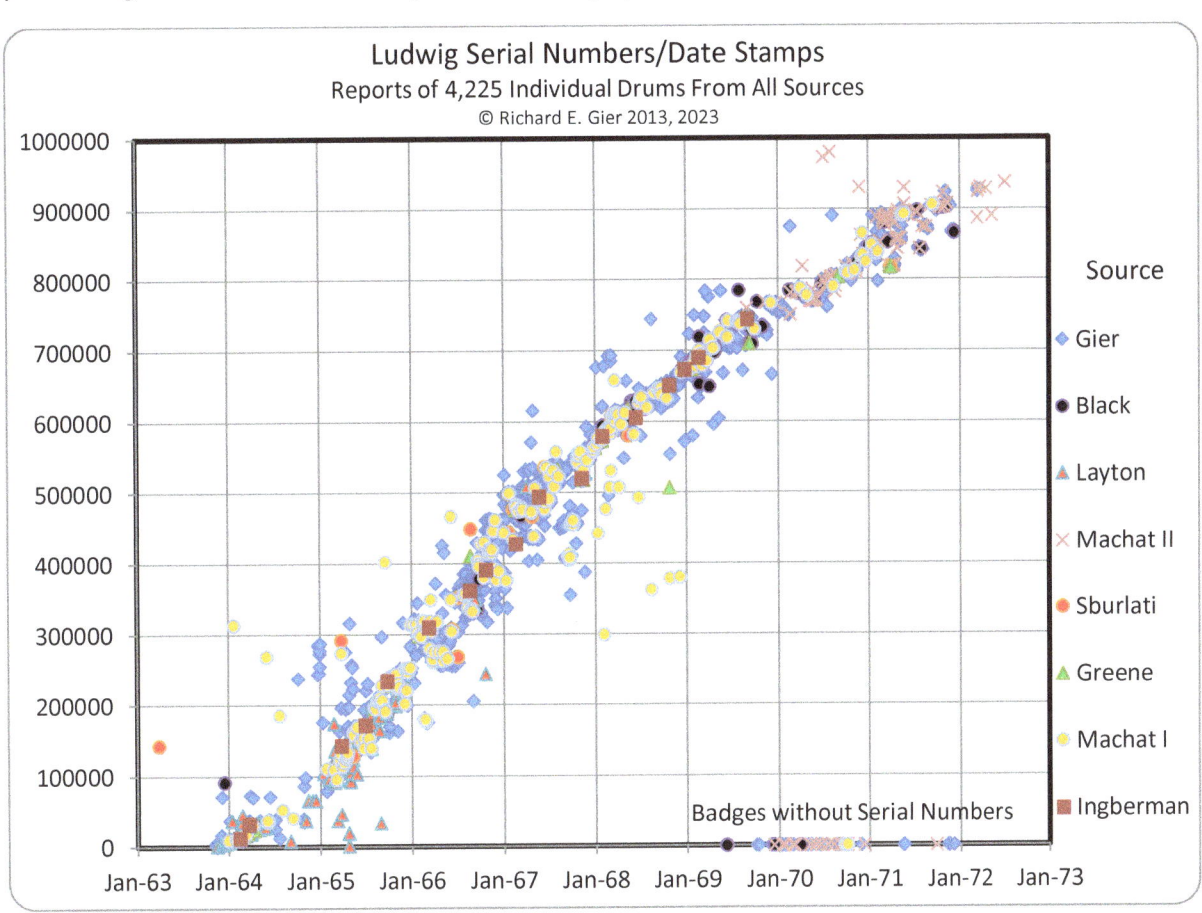

Graph 5 – Serial Numbers/Date Stamps from All Sources

---

[19] Those drums with only a year indicated are not considered precise enough for this study.
[20] Thirty-six of Machat's drums appear on Machat's second list or on lists from Sburlati, Greene and the author.

### B. Date Guide for Main Line Ludwig Drums Manufactured 1972-1984

Vintage Ludwig drums lack date stamps after about mid-1972, so a different approach is employed in order to address the years 1972-1984. Because Sburlati's dates are estimates and Cook relied upon Sburlati's information, a new guide is created without reference to those published resources. The serial numbers actually used by Ludwig are identified and then divided evenly over the corresponding date range. The start point is established using some of the latest date stamps recorded - May 1972 on drums with serial numbers in the 927000 range. The end point is established using 1984 as the date of the relocation to Monroe, North Carolina, and 3140000 as the first serial number used on a badge indicating Monroe as the manufacturing location. A relatively straight line between these end points is then drawn, acknowledging the gaps in serial numbers from 1400000 to 1500000 and again from 2300000 through 3000000, which were not used by Ludwig.[21] Graph 6 presents the dating guide for 1972 – 1984.

It should come as no surprise that the 1972-1984 guide comes with the caution that it does not produce precise date estimates. While it is an improvement over the published resources for the 1970s drums with Blue/Olive badges, it is still capable of providing only an approximate year of manufacture. It should not be used to support estimates more precise than a year. However, when coupled with the information about the Blue/Olive badge era contained in Part III, it offers ample justification to abandon the overuse of 1976 as the year of manufacture for most Blue/Olive badge drums.

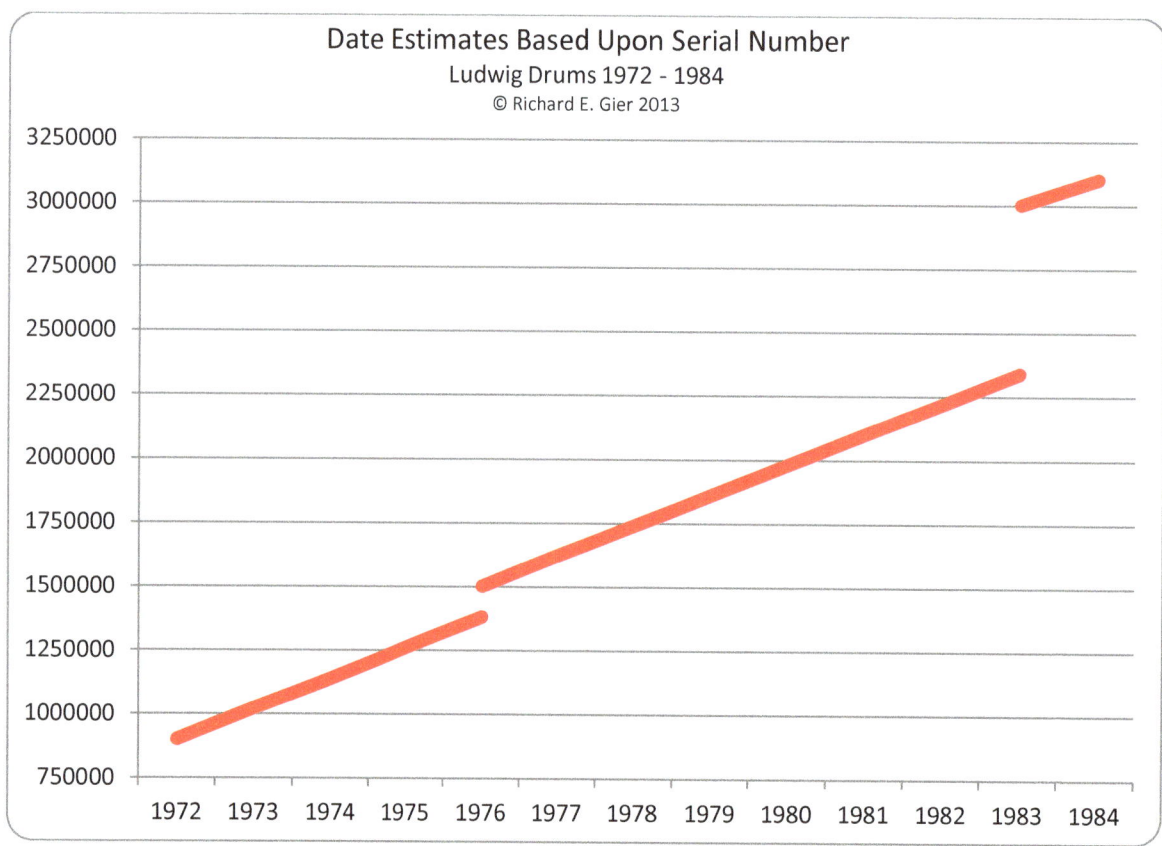

Graph 6 – Serial Number Date Guide for 1972-1984

---

[21] Specific information about serial numbers used, date range covered and manufacturing locations is included in Part III.

## PART III – LINKING PHYSICAL CHARACTERISTICS TO SERIAL NUMBERS AND DATE

Part III explores and establishes correlations between serial numbers, date stamps and changes in physical characteristics including hardware and finishes. This effort also answers some frequently debated questions about when certain changes in hardware occurred. While not every feature on every drum encountered can be easily explained, general expectations are established regarding what hardware and features an untouched, factory-original drum should possess. Production variations and post-factory modifications disrupt our sense of when particular changes in badges, interior coatings, and hardware occurred, but review of enough drums permits some culling of outlying data points and produces a reasonable estimation of serial number or date ranges for each change. It should be kept in mind that these serial number and date ranges are only estimates – their endpoints do not establish absolute boundaries. In addition to the drums discussed in Part II above, information from non-date stamped drums greatly expands the pool of resources for this portion of the study. To develop and support the following observations, information from a total of more than 16,700 main line drums is reviewed – 15,239 drums collected by the author and an additional 1,466 drums gathered by others.

### A. Badges

From 1963 through 1984 Ludwig used eight different badge designs on its main line drums. Some of these designs received additional modifications. Although Ludwig Drum Co. and its predecessors used keystone-shaped badges as early as 1937, the design that first received serial numbers made its debut in about October 1960. It is initially introduced without a serial number and is referred to as the "pre-serial number Keystone badge." After a few years, a serial number is added at the top of the badge. This version of the Keystone Badge ("K1") does not possess the "Circle R" symbol (®) which would be used to indicate that the trademark is registered. The K1 badge with serial number appears on drums date stamped as early as October 1963. The second version of the Keystone Badge ("K2") displays the Circle R symbol to the right of the letter "g" in Ludwig. The transition between K1 and K2 designs occurs in about 1964 at around serial number 59500.[22] This transition appears to have been absolute, with no known overlap of serial numbers between K1 and K2 badge designs. K2 badges display serial numbers as high as about 749000.[23] Few make a distinction between K1 and K2 badges, so these together are often referred to as the small Keystone Badge.

Figure 1 – K1 - Keystone Badge without ®

Figure 2 – K2 - Keystone Badge with ®

---

[22] K1 badges are reported with serial numbers as high as 59171 while K2 badges are reported with serial numbers as low as 59629.
[23] The highest recorded serial number on a K2 badge is 748987. One report of a K2 badge with serial number 749101 described in the first edition of this guide has been reviewed and determined to be 748101.

Four versions of the Blue/Olive Badge followed, using serial numbers from about 749000 to about 3140000.[24] The first is the Pointed Corner Blue/Olive Badge ("BO1"). It has a parallelogram shape with pointed corners at the top right and bottom left and rounded corners at top left and bottom right. It has blue and olive colored blocks at the top of the badge. It uses a new logo showing the name Ludwig in block letters with the letters L and G joined together underneath. This version of the badge does not contain the "Circle R" symbol indicating trademark registration.[25] This Pointed Corner Badge received serial numbers from about 749000 through about 945000.[26] The BO1 badge is reported on shells date stamped as early as August 1969, but seems to be prevalent on shells dated after December 1969. It ceased being used in about 1972.

The second version of Blue/Olive Badge is the same basic design as the first, but has the ® added above the letter G in Ludwig ("BO2"). The addition of the registration symbol occurred at about serial number 945000.[27] The BO2 badge continued through about serial number 2230000, with an apparent gap of unused serial numbers between about 1390000 and 1500000. The BO2 badge does not emerge until after Ludwig discontinues providing a date indicator on its drums, but it likely made its appearance some time in 1972. Few make a distinction between BO1 and BO2 badges, which are generally grouped together as "Pointy B/O" or "Pointed Corner B/O" badges.

Figure 3 - BO1 - Pointed Corner B/O Badge without ®    Figure 4 - BO2 - Pointed Corner B/O Badge with ®

The third version of Blue/Olive badge is the same basic design as the BO2, but has the pointed corners rounded off ("BO3"). The Rounded Corner Blue/Olive Badge appears at about serial number 1860000 and continues through about serial number 2300000.[28] There is significant overlap of the BO2 and BO3 from serial numbers 1860000 through 2230000, as either badge version might be present in this range. The period of overlap spans multiple production years. The Pointed Corner Badge (BO2) dominates the earlier portion of that range while the Rounded Corner Badge (BO3) dominates during the later portion, with the middle of the transition occurring at around serial number 2000000. It appears that many of the earlier Rounded Corner badges were modified after their original stamping to remove the pointed corners. Although the BO2 and BO3 badges are the same design cut a different way, they receive treatment as separate versions of the badge.

Following a second gap where serial numbers between about 2300000 and 3000000 are not used, a fourth version of the Blue/Olive badge emerges. The Round Corner Blue/Olive Badge ("BO4") starts at

---

[24] The lowest and highest serial numbers recorded thus far which are considered reliable are 749026 and 3139497.
[25] The trademark application for the new logo design declares March 28, 1969 as the date of first use and June 1, 1969 as the date of first use in commerce, but for some reason registration was not sought until May 16, 1979 and not granted until February 10, 1981.
[26] The highest recorded serial number on a BO1 Badge is 945384.
[27] The lowest recorded serial number on a BO2 Badge (with ®) is 945071.
[28] The lowest and highest serial numbers recorded on BO3 badges are 1865670 and 2284060.

serial number 3000000 and continues through about 3140000.[29] In addition to corners that are rounded, a thin black outline surrounds the serial number. The black line forms a parallelogram with the lower right corner rounded. This style of badge is best distinguished from the BO3 Rounded Corner Badge by the black outline around a serial number above 3000000. Many do not distinguish between the BO3 and BO4, grouping them together as "Round B/O" or "Round Corner B/O Badges."

Figure 5 - BO3 - Rounded Corner B/O Badge

Figure 6 – BO4 - Round Corner B/O Badge

**MYTH -** Ludwig serial numbers indicate the exact number of drums produced during different eras.
**TRUTH –** Due to damaged and unused badges, blocks of skipped serial numbers, use of badges without serial numbers and drums without badges, Ludwig serial numbers do not reflect production volume.

The seventh and eighth badge styles represent a return to the keystone shape, but these versions are considerably larger than the Keystone badge of the 1960s. These larger Keystone badges appeared first at about serial number 3090000. The first of these indicates manufacture in Chicago ("K3" or "Large Keystone - Chicago") and the second indicates manufacture in Monroe, NC ("K4" or "Large Keystone - Monroe"). K3 badges are recorded between about 3090000 and 3140000.[30] As noted above, the BO4 badge remained in use up through about serial number 3140000, so some potential for overlap with the K3 badge exists. No specific instance of duplicate serial numbers between BO4 and K3 badges is recorded thus far. It appears that the BO4 badge is used primarily on lower level drums while the K3 is used on higher end models. Some K3 badges possess no serial numbers, but it is unclear whether these blank K3 badges were among the first or last of this style of badge or appeared somewhere in between. K4 badges are recorded from about 3140000[31] and continued up from there, but few examples are recorded as part of this effort, as these extend past the time period of study.

Figure 7 - Large Keystone - Chicago Badge
(Kevin Oppendike)

Figure 8 - Large Keystone - Monroe Badge
(Kevin Oppendike)

---

[29] The highest serial number recorded thus far on a BO4 badge is 3139497.
[30] The lowest and highest serial numbers recorded are 3093743 and 3141098.
[31] The lowest serial number recorded is 3141879.

In an interesting and confusing twist, Ludwig reissued the B/O badge in the late 2000s. The reissued B/O badge looks very similar to the BO4, but some have the additional language "MADE IN USA" under the serial number inside the black outline. For its reissued B/O badges, Ludwig returned to serial numbers starting at about 3140000, which is where they left off with the BO4 badge in the 1980s. It seems likely that some of serial numbers used on K4 badges in the 1980s are duplicated on reissued B/O badges in the 2000s, since both appear to have started in the 3140000 range. Insufficient information is available to confirm this theory. The similarities between BO4 and the reissued B/O badge and the return to the serial number range used in the 1980s make it difficult for many to easily distinguish between the reissues and their vintage originals. Serial number 3140000 should be a reliable cutoff point between the two.

Although additional badge styles are used after those discussed here, study of the later eras of Ludwig is left to someone with a greater interest in modern drums. The Large Keystone badge is useful for this study as the end of Chicago production and the move to Monroe, NC occurred in 1984.[32] Where date stamps are not present, a date indicator like this establishes a date on the timeline when certain serial numbers were used.

**Table 1**
**Badge Styles on Main Line Drums**
© Richard E. Gier, 2013, 2023

| Badge Style | Serial Number Range | Date Range |
|---|---|---|
| K1 - Keystone without ® | 1 to 59500 | NOV 1963 to ~Mid 1964 |
| K2 - Keystone with ® | 59500 to 749000 | ~Mid 1964 to NOV 1969 |
| BO1 - Pointed Corner B/O without ® | 749000 to 945000 | NOV 1969 to ~1972 |
| BO2 - Pointed Corner B/O with ® | 945000 to 2230000 | ~1972 to ~1981 |
| BO3 - Rounded Corner B/O | 1880000 to 2300000 | Late 1970s to ~1982 |
| BO4 - Round Corner B/O | 3000000 to 3140000 | ~1982 to 1984 |
| K3 - Large Keystone – Chicago | 3090000 to 3140000 | ~1983 to 1984 |
| K4 - Large Keystone – Monroe | 3140000 to higher | 1984 to later |

**B. Interior Finish**

Ludwig uses different interior finishes on its drum shells over time. Prior to the introduction of serial numbers, the shells have unfinished wood interiors. A white paint described as an "exclusive Resa-Cote spray interior finish" is introduced in the early 1960s. Some sets with pre-serial number Keystone badges contain drums with a mix of unfinished and Resa-Cote interiors. By the time serial numbers are in use in late 1963, the vast majority of drums have Resa-Cote interior finishes. The vast majority of Resa-Cote interiors appear with date stamps on or before March 28, 1968. Serial numbers on shells with Resa-Cote interiors tend to be 610000 or lower. A handful of drums with later dates and higher serial numbers are recorded. For example, collector Bun E. Carlos reported a Psych Red Jazz Festival oddity with serial number 816947 and date stamp April 21, 1971 with a Resa-Cote interior and a BO1 Badge.[33]

---

[32] Ludwig employee Jim Catalano states that the move to Monroe occurred in 1984. Cook, at p. 55. The move is dated to 1984 at the Conn-Selmer website as well. https://www.ludwig-drums.com/en-us/ludwig/about, accessed February 14, 2023.

[33] This drum was featured in Not So Modern Drummer in the Bun E. Carlos' Ludwig Collection Spotlight, http://notsomoderndrummer.com/bun-e-carlos.html, June 2012. Speculation about the reasons for the unusual combination of characteristics of this drum is included in the article.

Figure 9 - Resa-Cote Interior    Figure 10 – Clear Lacquer Interior    Figure 11 – Lud-Cote Interior

In 1968, the Resa-Cote interior is replaced with an "exclusive hot clear lacquer spray."[34] This Clear interior is typically seen on drums with date stamps from MAR 28 1968 and later, and serial numbers above 610000. The earliest date stamp recorded with a Clear interior is FEB 5 1968. The lowest reported serial number on a drum with a Clear interior is 551681. It is commonly believed that the date stamping operation was a part of the shell manufacturing operation. If true, it follows that the change from Resa-Cote to Clear interior would appear abrupt as far as date stamps go. Because badges are attached at a later step in the drum assembly, and are already being used in non-sequential order, the relationship between interior finish and serial number would be expected to be more varied. Both situations appear to be present. The overwhelming majority of drums with Resa-Cote interiors have earlier date stamps than drums with Clear interiors. There is a larger overlap with serial numbers, with some lower serial numbers appearing on drums with Clear interiors and some higher serial numbers appearing on drums with Resa-Cote interiors. While some of the overlap may be the result of badges switched during later restoration efforts, most appears to be the result of Ludwig's lack of strict orderly use of serial numbered badges.

The third interior finish of the serial number era is the Lud-Cote finish, a gray-based, speckled paint similar to automotive trunk paint. The Lud-Cote interior finish is introduced by Ludwig on its Standard line of drums, but it is listed under the brand name Granitone in the 1968 Standard catalog.[35] The Lud-Cote name first appeared in the 1971 main line catalog. The earliest recorded date stamp on a main line drum with a Lud-Cote interior is APR 19 1971. It appears that the last main line drum with a gray-based Lud-Cote interior was made in about 1979.[36] It is difficult to detect a date stamp on the Lud-Cote interior and few are reported, so the date range should be considered a very rough estimate. Drums with both Clear and Lud-Cote interiors are seen through the majority of the 1970s. There does not seem to be a detectible pattern for which finish a drum would receive during that time, but more appear to have received Clear than Lud-Cote interior finishes.

**Table 2**
**Interior Finish Styles on Main Line Drums**
© Richard E. Gier, 2013, 2023

| Interior Finish | Serial Number Range | Date Range |
|---|---|---|
| Resa-Cote | 0 to ~610000 | NOV 1963 to MAR 1968 |
| Clear | ~610000 to higher | APR 1968 to later |
| Lud-Cote | ~816000 to ~1810000 | ~1971 to ~1979 |

---

[34] This language appears in the 1971 catalog.
[35] The name Lud-Cote was also used for a brown-based speckled paint used on second line drums in the 1980s.
[36] The lowest serial number recorded in this effort on a main line drum with a Lud-Cote interior is 816350, while the highest is 1812133.

## C. Number of Plies in Shell

During the 1960s and much of the 1970s, Ludwig wood shells are made of three plies of wood with reinforcing rings to provide stability. The shells are usually constructed with mahogany/poplar/mahogany or maple/poplar/maple layers. In the mid to late 1970s, Ludwig shifted to a six ply shell without reinforcing rings. This study does not delve into the details of Ludwig's shell construction, but the approximate transition point from 3 ply to 6 ply shells is identified as occurring in the 1635000 serial number range in about the 1977 time frame. As with other changes in physical characteristics linked to serial number ranges, this estimate is subject to the variability of Ludwig's production practices.

Figure 12 – 3 Ply Shell

Figure 13 – 6 ply Shell

**Table 3**
**Number of Plies in Shell on Main Line Drums**
© Richard E. Gier, 2013, 2023

| Number of Plies | Serial Number Range | Date Range |
|---|---|---|
| 3 | 0 to ~1635000 | NOV 1963 to ~1977 |
| 6 | ~1635000 to higher | ~1977 to later |

## D. Tone Controls

Ludwig used a number of different tone controls or mufflers during the period studied. Generally, only the batter side has a tone control, but some drums have tone controls on both batter and resonant sides. In the very early 1960s, prior to the introduction of serial numbers, Ludwig was using the model P-4066 tone control with a relatively small (3/4" diameter) knurled round adjusting knob and a gray round felt pad ("Small Knob Tone Control").

Figure 14 - Small Knob Tone Control

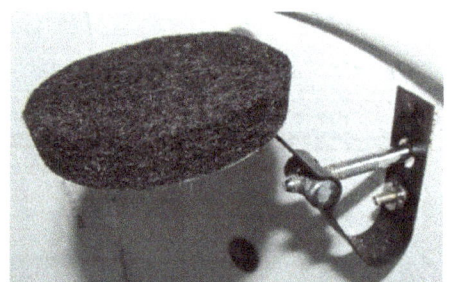
Figure 15 – Small Knob Tone Control – Internal

In about 1962, Ludwig introduced the model P-4067 tone control which had a long handle and a rectangular felt pad ("Baseball Bat Tone Control"). When the serial number era started in late 1963, both

Small Knob and Baseball Bat Tone Controls are seen, with the Small Knob Tone Control generally seen on marching drums. Two different color felts are used on Baseball Bat Tone Controls, with the earlier ones receiving red felt and the later ones possessing white. The Red Felt Baseball Bat Tone Control is seen consistently on drums with serial numbers from the beginning through about 110000. They are present on the drums with the earliest date stamps through about early March 1965.[37] Above about serial number 110000 and after date stamp MAR 5 1965, the White Felt Baseball Bat Tone Control is consistently used.[38]

Figure 16 - Baseball Bat Tone Control

Figure 17 - Red Felt

Figure 18 - White Felt

One of vintage drum enthusiast Mike Layton's goals was to identify the transition point between red and white felts on baseball bat tone controls. Analysis of Layton's information and additional reports collected for this project confirms the March/April 1965 time frame and 110000 serial number range as estimates for the transition point. Nearly fifty years later it cannot be said that there is a precise point where the transition occurred, but this represents the best available estimate.

There is significant overlap of felt color. The variability seen in the serial number/date stamp relationship discussed in Part II is only further amplified when an additional variable is introduced. Post-factory modifications and inaccurate drum restorations may add more layers of variation. Anecdotally, many of the red felt tone controls seen on drums with high serial numbers and late date stamps, and conversely, white felt tone controls on drums with low serial numbers and early date stamps, are on drums which appear to be modified in other ways. Many are offered by volume sellers with access to spare parts and with reputations for glossing over inconsistencies in their descriptions. While one should not merely attempt to explain away drums which do not fit the typical, it is difficult to place much weight on the originality of the tone control felt color when they are easily switched.

The Baseball Bat Tone Control continues in use until about February 1968 and the 575000 serial number range. Small Knob Tone Controls appear sporadically on a variety of models, especially marching drums, throughout the Baseball Bat era. The Small Knob Tone Control resurfaces in large number when the Baseball Bat Tone Control is discontinued in the February 1968 time frame, appearing mainly on Acrolite snare models and marching drums.

Also in 1968, the model 4066-2 tone control with a larger 1" diameter adjusting knob is introduced. It is initially used on most non-marching drums and eventually on all drums with tone controls. This Large Knob Tone Control appears on drums with serial numbers as low as 563976 and date stamps as early as JAN 25 1968, but become the norm by about serial number 575000. Multiple versions

---

[37] The highest reliable report of a serial number recorded on a drum which had a Red Felt Baseball Bat Tone Control is 126072. The latest reliable report of a date stamp recorded on a drum with a Red Felt Baseball Bat Tone Control is April 7, 1965.

[38] The earliest report of a White Felt Baseball Bat Tone Control which seems reliable has a date stamp of February 11, 1965. The lowest reported serial number for a White Felt Baseball Bat Tone Control which seems reliable is 74182.

of the Large Knob Tone Control are used from the late 1960s through the 1980s. They initially have a single mount bolt located below the tone control knob. This is moved to above the knob in about the 1700000 serial number range in about 1977-78. The initial Vistalite drums in the early 1970s had Large Knob Tone Controls with single mount bolts, initially below and later above the knob, and black colored round felts. Near serial number 1350000, many Vistalites began to receive tone controls with three mount bolts which were initially located below the knob. These were later shifted to above the knob. Transition points, particularly on Vistalites, are not very precise and significant overlap in bolt number and location exist. There were also changes in the washers and spacers used with the various Large Knob Tone Controls. Paolo Sburlati describes changes in the Large Knob Tone Controls, particularly with the Vistalite models.[39]

Figures 19 & 20 - Large Knob Tone Control with Single Mount Bolt Below and Above Knob

Figure 21 – Large Round Knob Tone Control with One Mount Bolt Below Knob

Figure 22 - Large Round Knob Tone Control with Three Mount Bolts Below Knob

**Table 4**
**Tone Control Styles on Main Line Drums**
© Richard E. Gier, 2013, 2023

| Tone Control Style | Serial Number Range | Date Range |
|---|---|---|
| Small Knob | Very low | NOV 1963 to 1964 |
| Red Felt Baseball Bat | 0 to 110000 | NOV 1963 to MAR 1965 |
| White Felt Baseball Bat | 110000 to 575000 | MAR 1965 to FEB 1968 |
| Small Knob Reprise | 570000 to 745000 | FEB 1968 to ~1970 |
| Large Knob 1 bolt below knob | 575000 to ~1700000 | FEB 1968 to ~1977-78 |
| Large Knob 1 bolt above knob | ~1700000 to higher | ~1977-78 to later |

---

[39] Sburlati, p 176.

Tone control placement also varied through the years. During the 1960s and early 1970s, most drums had tone controls located one or two panels away from the badge. Marching drums had tone controls directly above the badges. Around 1975 and in serial number range 1190000-1250000, it became the norm to place tone controls for mounted toms directly above the badge.[40] Snares and floor toms continued to have badges and tone controls on separate panels from the badge. In addition, as the 1970s advanced, many drums, initially concert toms and later involving many models, did not possess tone controls at all. Definitive dates for the discontinuation of tone controls are not determined in this study.

Figure 23 - Large Knob Tone Control Located Above Badge

### E. Date Indicator

When a date is indicated on a main line drum, it takes one of three forms: a date stamp placed on the interior of the shell, a date stamp placed on a paper label inside the shell, or a Date Code placed on a paper label inside the shell. It seems generally accepted in the vintage drum community that the date indicators were applied at the time of shell manufacture. However, it is also possible that the date stamp was a part of the assembly process, as indicated by Dick Schory, who worked for Ludwig from the late 1950s through 1971.[41] It seems possible that Ludwig's procedure may have been altered in the later 1960s and early 1970s.[42] There is a general pattern for when each type of date indication was used.

Figure 24 - Date Stamp – Red Ink                    Figure 25 - Date Stamp - Black Ink

*1. Date Stamp.* By the time Ludwig began imprinting serial numbers in late 1963, the practice of stamping the shells with a date is already well established. The format is "JAN 01 1900" with a three-letter month, two digit date and four digit year. The initial date stamps for serialized drums are in red ink. By about March 1965, at about serial number 110000, black ink is added to the mix. From that point until about September 1965 and serial number 207000, date stamps appear in red or black ink. Thereafter, black ink

---

[40] VintageDrumForum.com member Drumguy1988 shared his research into this particular issue.
[41] Mr. Schory was asked at the 2018 Chicago Drum Show and he indicated that the date stamps were applied at assembly. I did not seek clarification if this was the procedure always used by Ludwig.
[42] Bun E. Carlos' Psych Red Jazz Festival with a 1971 date stamp on a shell with Resa-Cote interior finish mentioned in an earlier footnote and its accompanying explanation supports this theory.

is used almost exclusively for date stamps. This continues through about APR 13 1971 and about serial number 894000. There is overlap before and after these points, but that provides a rough range for the ink colors used for date stamps.

*2. Date Stamps on Paper Label.* On about APR 15 1971, and about serial number 850000 (although a few serial numbers as low as the 816000 range are reported), Ludwig began to place paper labels in the inside of its shells. These paper labels had spaces for both a date and a model number. The dates were still indicated in black ink with the same type of stamp used on the shells. This practice continued on wood shell drums through May 1971 and on metal shell drums through January 1972 and about serial number 927000.[43]

Figure 26 – Paper Label with Date Stamp

Figure 27 – Paper Label with Date Code (Mike Machat)

*3. Date Codes on Paper Label.* Some paper labels display a different type of number in the space for the date. This Date Code is explored more fully in Part V of this paper, but the Date Code was used from about June 1971- April 1972. Date Codes first appeared on wood shelled drums in about June 1971 and metal shell drums in about January 1972. The reported serial numbers on main line drums with paper labels with Date Codes spans from 825829 to 938639. There is significant overlap in serial numbers on drums receiving labels with date stamps and those receiving labels with Date Codes, as both were used for about seven months.

**Table 5**
**Date Indicator Styles on Main Line Drums**
© Richard E. Gier, 2013, 2023

| Date Range | Serial Number Range | Date Indicator |
|---|---|---|
| NOV 1963 to MAR 1965 | 0 to 110000 | Red Ink Stamp |
| MAR 1965 to SEP 1965 | 110000 to 207000 | Red or Black Ink Stamp |
| SEP 1965 to APR 1971 | 207000 to 894000 | Black Ink Stamp |
| APR 1971 to MAY 1971 | 816000[44] to 890000 | Paper Label - Black Ink Stamp - Wood Shells |
| JUN 1971 to APR 1972 | 850000 to 938000 | Paper Label - Date Code - Wood Shells |
| APR 1971 to JAN 1972 | 816000 to 924000 | Paper Label – Black Ink Stamp - Metal Shells |
| JAN 1972 to APR 1972 | 890000 to 938000 | Paper Label - Date Code - Metal Shells |
| APR 1972 to later | 924000 to higher | No Date Stamp or Paper Label |

---

[43] Machat reports two drums with much later date stamps, a drum stamped JUL 14 1972 with serial number 936724 and a drum date stamped MAY 24 1973 with serial number 984203. It is not known if these drums have labels or the dates are stamped on the shell.

[44] Complicating the analysis shown in Table 5 is Ludwig's sudden shift from serial numbers which had gradually risen to the 894000 range by late March 1971 to serial numbers in the 815000 – 821000 range for most of the month of April 1971. Ludwig resumed the use of higher serial numbers (850000s – 890000s) in late April 1971.

### F. Snare Throw-Offs

The majority of Ludwig main line snare drums made from 1963 to 1984 possess one of two models of throw-offs: the P-83 and multiple versions of the P-85. Super Sensitive, Classic and piccolo snare models received other types of throw-offs, which are not explored in this brief look at throw-off hardware. The P-83 and P-85 throw-offs are easily interchangeable because the mounting holes are the same distance apart, so new holes need to be drilled. As a result, many vintage snare drums no longer sport the throw they had when the left the factory. Despite this, observation of many drums permits the throw-off to be tracked over time and added to the list of physical characteristics which are linked to date and serial number.

The P-83 throw-off with a script logo is used from prior to the introduction of serial numbers until about March/April 1969 and about serial number range 680000 - 710000, when it was replaced with the P-85. The P-85 initially had a black faceplate with a block logo and 12 holes for snare attachment. The first style of P-85 is in use through about serial number 1070000 and about 1973/1974. The second style of P-85 retains the black faceplate, but reduces to two the number of holes for attaching the snare wires. The P-85 with two holes continues in use through the early 1980s. The twelve hole design resurfaces briefly in the 1980s, when one might encounter P-85 throw-offs with black faceplates with either two or twelve holes.

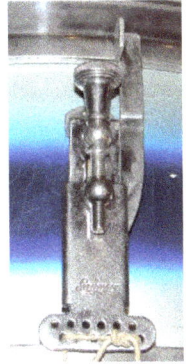  

Figure 28 - P-83     Figure 29 - P-85 Black Face/12 Holes     Figure 30 – P85 Black Face/2 Holes

Modern versions of the P-85 abandon the black faceplate in favor of chrome and change the snare attachment arrangement to a metal band attached to the throw-off with two bolts to accommodate snare tape rather than snare cord. When these are seen on older drums, they are replacements for the original P-83 or P-85s. The following table provides a summary of the serial number and date ranges observed for the different models of throw-offs.

**Table 6**
**Snare Throw-Off Styles on Main Line Drums**
© Richard E. Gier, 2013, 2023

| Throw-Off Style | Serial Number | Date Stamp / Range |
|---|---|---|
| P-83 | 0 to 710000 | NOV 1963 to MAR/APR 1969 |
| P-85 Black Face 12 Hole | 680000 to 1070000 | MAR/APR 1969 to ~1973 |
| P-85 Black Face 2 Hole | 1070000 to 2300000 | ~1973 to ~1982 |
| P-85 Black Face 2 or 12 Hole | 3000000 to higher | ~1982 to later |
| P-85 Chrome Face 2 Hole screw tightened strap | Modern Replacement | Modern Replacement |

### G. Riveted Wrap Seams

At one point Ludwig used rivets to secure the wrap seam on some of its wraps, apparently to answer wrap shrinkage issues. The vast majority of drums recorded as having riveted seams possess sparkle, pearl, silk or chrome wraps, but not cortex wraps. The riveted seams occurred in the serial number ranges of 1900000 - 2300000 and 3000000 - 3070000. This represents a span of 470,000 serial numbers, accounting for the gap of unused serial numbers between 2300000 and 3000000. Rivet use occurred in about the 1978 – 1982 time frame. Metal shelled drums did not have rivets, so only a fraction of the 460,0000 drums produced during this era have riveted wrap seams. These observations are subject to refinement as more information is gathered.

Figure 31 – Tom with Riveted Seam

### H. Anti-Galvanic Plating Markings on Chrome Shells

Ludwig used a variety of interior markings to indicate the use of an Anti-Galvanic plating process for its chrome-plated metal shells. These consisted of stamps and stickers applied by either the primary plating supplier, or Ludwig itself. An in-depth study of the timeline of these markings is summarized below.[45]

A total of 232 of the 1,500 chrome-plated main line drums in the database from 1968-1984 (the era when anti-galvanic stamps and stickers were used) are known to possess an identifiable Anti-Galvanic stamp or sticker. This creates a group of drums from which we can learn about Anti-Galvanic stamps and stickers and construct a timeline.

*1. A-G Stamp:* Stamps with capital letters "A" and "G" were introduced in about mid-1968 and used for about a year and a half until the end of 1969, with one report in January 1970. The stamp appears both with and without the A and G separated by a hyphen – "AG" and "A-G". (Both variations are grouped into a single title "AG" stamps for this article.) Black ink is used. Sometimes one letter is upside down relative to the other - "∀G" or "A-Ɔ". There are four additional examples of other stamps using the same size and font of letters in black ink, including BGA, EGA, G and GC. Other variations likely exist.

---

[45] Richard E. Gier, "Understanding Ludwig's Use of "Anti-Galvanic" Stamps and Stickers on Chrome Drums 1968 – 1984." July 28, 2021 https://gretschdrumdatingguide.com/other-projects.html and Not So Modern Drummer July 30, 2021 www.notsomoderndrummer.com/not-so-modern-drummer/2021/7/29/understanding-ludwigs-use-of-anti-galvanic-stamps-and-stickers-on-chrome-drums-1968-1984

Figure 32 - A-G Stamp (Supersonic Music)    Figure 33 - "RELIABLE ANTI-GALVANIC" Stamp (Midwest Drum)

*2. "RELIABLE ANTI-GALVANIC" Stamp:*  In very late 1969/early 1970, the "AG" Stamp was replaced with a new much larger stamp which contained the words "Reliable Anti-Galvanic."  It appears in black ink and is often stamped twice.  This stamp appears on drums with date stamps as early as December 1969 and on drums with Date Codes.  "Reliable" does not refer to the finishing process, but to the Reliable Plating Corporation, the company which provided the chrome finishing.

*3. White Rectangle "Reliable ANTI-GALVANIC Plating" Sticker:*  This particular variation is not well documented.  It is a white sticker with the words "Reliable ANTI-GALVANIC Plating" in blue ink.  One example has been documented, although undocumented reports of this label exist.  It is inappropriate to define serial number range or time frame where this sticker should occur with just one report, but the 1100985 serial number places this singular example in about 1974.

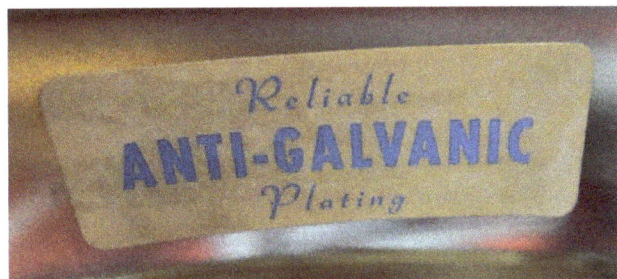

Figure 34 - Rectangular Sticker – (Richard Blanchard, Mrfathead Drums)

*4. Oval '"Reliable" ANTI-GALVANIC' blue sticker with white or gold letters*:  This additional sticker design is also not particularly common.  It is an oval-shaped sticker with a blue background and gold or white letters.  It displays the words "Reliable (in quotes) ANTI-GALVANIC".  Six examples are documented.

Figure 35 - Oval Sticker (Supersonic Music)    Figure 36 - Round Blue Ludaloy Sticker

*5. Round Blue Ludaloy Reliable Plating Sticker:* The final sticker was in use for many years and first appears in about 1976. It is round with a blue background and white lettering. This is the only stamp/sticker which indicates the shell material – Ludaloy. The presentation is a stylized design which mimics the block logo used by Ludwig beginning in the late 1960s. Along with the Ludaloy branding are the phrases "A RELIABLE Plating Process," "Corrosion Resistant" and "ANTI-GALVANIC FINISH." It appears that this sticker was in use until Ludwig relocated from Chicago to Monroe, North Carolina in about 1984. That move mostly ended the relationship between Ludwig and Reliable Plating.

**Table 7**
**Anti-Galvanic Plating Markings**
© Richard E. Gier, 2013, 2023

| Approximate Time Period | Approximate Serial Number Range | Stamp or Sticker Type |
|---|---|---|
| ~1958 to 1968 | Pre-serial – 620000 | None |
| 1968 to JAN 1970 | 620000 – 750000 | AG, GA, A-G, G-A Stamp |
| 1970 to- ~1975 | 756319 - 1207444 | "RELIABLE ANTI-GALVANIC" Stamp |
| ~1974 | 1100985 (one report) | Rectangular "Reliable ANTI-GALVANIC Plating" white sticker with blue letters |
| ~1985 | 1170023 – 1260485 | Oval "'Reliable' ANTI-GALVANIC" blue sticker with white or gold letters |
| ~1976 to 1980s | 1532560 – 3178025 | Round Blue Ludaloy Sticker |

Now that each of six physical characteristics has been examined separately, they are combined to create a chart which summarizes the changes in physical characteristics one can expect to find on main line Ludwig drums produced with serial numbers from 1963 – 1984. The characteristic that represents a change in each row is presented in **Bold**.

This summary comes with the caveats, warnings and limitations that are described in this paper. It does not produce guaranteed down-to-the-day estimates; it provides a general guide of the serial numbers and date stamps associated with particular physical characteristics of a typical vintage Ludwig drum. The end points of the serial number and date ranges are approximations - drums may exist outside of the ranges which are factory original and unaltered. As discussed above and by the authors of many of the published guides, variations existed in Ludwig's manufacture of drums which may explain an atypical feature. However, when an unusual drum is encountered, one should look for indications of alteration and inquire about the drum's history. One may never know for sure about the authenticity of a vintage drum, but with this information should be able to make a better educated guess.

**Table 8**
**Summary of Changes for Main Line Ludwig Drums**
© Richard E. Gier, 2013, 2023

| Approximate Serial No. | Date | Date Style | Badge Style | Shell | Tone Control | Throw-Off |
|---|---|---|---|---|---|---|
| **0 – 59500** | NOV 1963 – Mid 1964 | Red Stamp | K1 Keystone | Resa-Cote 3-ply | Red Felt Baseball Bat | P-83 |
| 59500 - 110000 | Mid 1964 - MAR 1965 | Red Stamp | **K2 Keystone** | Resa-Cote 3-ply | Red Felt Baseball Bat | P-83 |
| 110000 - 207000 | MAR 1965 - SEP 1965 | **Red or Black Stamp** | K2 Keystone | Resa-Cote 3-ply | **White Felt Baseball Bat** | P-83 |
| 207000 - 575000 | SEP 1965 – FEB 1968 | **Black Stamp** | K2 Keystone | Resa-Cote 3-ply | White Felt Baseball Bat | P-83 |
| 570000 – 610000 | FEB 1968 – MAR 1968 | Black Stamp | K2 Keystone | Resa-Cote 3-ply | **Small or Large Knob** | P-83 |
| 610000 - 687000 | MAR 1968 - APR 1969 | Black Stamp | K2 Keystone | **Clear 3-ply** | Large Knob | P-83 |
| 687000 - 749000 | APR 1969 - NOV 1969 | Black Stamp | K2 Keystone | Clear 3-ply | Large Knob | **P-85 Black Face 12 hole** |
| 749000 – 840000 | DEC 1969 - APR 1971 | Black Stamp | **BO1 Pointed Corner B/O without ®** | Clear 3-ply | Large Knob | P-85 Black Face 12 hole |
| 840000 – 850000 | APR 1971 – ~1971 | **Paper Label** | BO1 Pointed Corner B/O without ® | Clear 3-ply | Large Knob | P-85 Black Face 12 hole |
| 850000 - 940000 - | ~1971 – APR 1972 | Paper Label | BO1 Pointed Corner B/O without ® | **Lud-Cote** and Clear 3-ply | Large Knob | P-85 Black Face 12 hole |
| 940000 - 945000 | ~1972 | **No Date Stamps** | BO1 Pointed Corner B/O without ® | Lud-Cote and Clear 3-ply | Large Knob | P-85 Black Face 12 hole |
| 945000 - 1070000 | ~1972 – ~1973 | No Date Stamps | **BO2 Pointed Corner B/O with ®** | Lud-Cote and Clear 3-ply | Large Knob | P-85 Black Face 12 hole |
| 1070000 - 1390000 | ~1973 – ~1976 | No Date Stamps | BO2 Pointed Corner B/O with ® | Lud-Cote and Clear 3-ply | Large Knob | **P-85 Black Face 2 hole** |
| 1390000 - 1500000 | **THESE** | **SERIAL** | **NUMBERS** | **WERE** | **NOT** | **USED** |
| 1500000 - 1620000 | ~1976 | No Date Stamps | BO2 Pointed Corner B/O with ® | Lud-Cote and Clear 3-ply | Large Knob | P-85 Black Face 2 hole |
| 1620000 - 1635000 | ~1977 | No Date Stamps | BO2 Pointed Corner B/O with ® | **Clear 3-ply** | Large Knob | P-85 Black Face 2 hole |
| 1635000 - 1880000 | ~1977 – ~1978 | No Date Stamps | BO2 Pointed Corner B/O with ® | Clear **6-ply** | Large Knob | P-85 Black Face 2 hole |

## Table 8 (continued)
## Summary of Changes for Main Line Ludwig Drums
© Richard E. Gier, 2013, 2023

| Approximate Serial No. | Date | Date Style | Badge Style | Shell | Tone Control | Throw-Off |
|---|---|---|---|---|---|---|
| 1880000 - 2300000 | ~1978 – ~1982 | No Date Stamps | BO2 Pointed Corner B/O with ® or **BO3 Rounded Pointed Corner B/O** | Clear 6-ply | Large Knob | P-85 Black Face 2 hole |
| 2300000 – 3000000 | **THESE** | **SERIAL** | **NUMBERS** | **WERE** | **NOT** | **USED** |
| 3000000 - 3090000 | ~1982 | No Date Stamps | **BO4 Round Corner B/O Only** | Clear 6-ply | Large Knob | **P-85 Black Face 2 or 12 hole** |
| 3090000 - 3140000 | ~1983 – ~1984 | No Date Stamps | BO4 Round Corner B/O **and K1 - Large Keystone – Chicago** | Clear 6-ply | Large Knob | P-85 Black Face 2 or 12 hole |
| 3140000 - on | ~1984 – on | No Date Stamps | **K2 - Large Keystone - Monroe** | Clear 6-ply | Large Knob | P-85 Black Face 2 or 12 hole |

**MYTH** - A drum without the typical combination of serial number, date stamp and physical characteristics is a prototype, "transition," endorser or special-order drum that is rare and valuable. **TRUTH** – It is more likely that such a drum possesses replacement parts or just received a peculiar combination of parts at that factory that do not greatly increase its value.

## PART IV - DATING GUIDE FOR LUDWIG STANDARD DRUMS 1968-1973

From 1968 through about 1973, Ludwig produced drums under the Standard brand name, marketing them as a second line of drums for the cost-conscious. Standards receive the same 3-ply shells as the more valued main line drums, yet offer unique wraps and different hardware. Some seeking the classic vintage Ludwig sound opt for the more affordable Standards. Heightened interest in Standards is accompanied with increased desire for information about them. However, all that is known by most vintage drum enthusiasts is that Standards did not use the same serial number system.[46] Part IV presents a serial number-based dating guide for Ludwig Standards and reports information on other characteristics of these long-overlooked drums.[47]

---

[46] On https://www.vintagedrumguide.com/serial_numbers.html (visited February 15, 2023), three different serial number-based guides for main line Ludwigs are provided, but a picture of a Standard badge is accompanied with the statement: "If you have this badge you can't use the serial number guides below."

[47] Ludwig produced other second line drums Ludwig in later years, including a revival of the Standard moniker (as Standard Line) in the 1980s. Only Standards produced from the late 1960s through the early 1970s are addressed here.

Figure 37 – Ludwig Standard Set (Kevin Oppendike)    Figure 38 - Ludwig Standard Snare Drum

### A. Description of Approach

As demonstrated above, developing a serial-number based dating guide relies upon the presence of both serial numbers and an indicator of a drum's date of manufacture or purchase. With Standards, serial numbers are generally present, but the date indicators are often not available. Therefore, the goal is to correlate serial numbers to known dates so that the age of Standard drums without date indicators can be estimated based upon serial numbers alone. Other physical characteristics of the drums can offer additional insight and help to support the dating approach developed based upon the serial numbers.

Information collected on Standards includes: serial number, date stamp or date code, interior finish, exterior wrap, existence of a label, type of drum, dimensions, configuration of set (if part of a set), style of throw-off (if snare) and model number. Sources of information include internet auction listings, posts on internet drum forums, reports from drum owners and personal inspection of available drums. As with the data collection for the main line drums, a diligent attempt is made to include only reliable information. This may result in the exclusion of otherwise valid data as suspect drums are culled from the database. The database of Standard drums contains 1,360 entries.

### B. Serial Numbers

Serial numbers are stamped into metal badges which are affixed to the drums with grommets, although several badges without serial numbers are also recorded. It appears that all Standard drums were issued badges, although not all of those badges are present or completely intact today. Standards do not utilize the same serial number sequence as the main line Keystone and Blue/Olive badge drums. Based upon the data collected to date, about 95,000 Standard serial numbers were created, numbering from about 1000 to about 96000. One drum with a three digit serial number and several in the 1XXX range are reported. The highest Standard serial number recorded thus far is 95926. Collected serial numbers appear to be fairly evenly distributed in the span of approximately 95,000 numbers, with no major gaps evident. It is not assumed that Ludwig issued or applied serial numbers in strict numerical order. Although this has not been documented, the production procedure may have mirrored the process reportedly utilized on main line drums which reportedly involved dumping badges into bins and then grabbing them one at a time when needed.[48] As with main line drums, this practice would introduce a variation in the order of issuance of badge numbers.

---

[48] Cook, at p. 210, and Ingberman, at p. 128.

Figure 39 - Standard Badge with Serial Number

### C. Date Indicators

As with the main Line drums, when a date is indicated on a Standard drum, it takes one of three forms: a date stamp placed on the interior of the shell, a date stamp placed on a paper label inside the shell, or a Date Code placed on a paper label inside the shell. It is not certain when in the production process the date indicator is added, whether when the shell is manufactured or the drum is assembled. However, like with the main line drums, there is a general pattern for when each type of date indication is used.

*1. Date Stamps on Shell* Many earlier Standards have dates stamped inside their shells. It is in the same "JAN 01 1900" format used on the main line drums and generally in black ink, although some are in red.[49] Also like their main line brethren, whether a date stamp is present and readable on a Standard drum today seems dependent upon a number of factors. First is whether it received a date stamp in the first place. It appears that many did not. Second is whether the date stamp with its water-soluble ink survives intact today. Third, as more fully explored below, many Standards have the additional complicating factor of possessing Granitone interior finishes upon which date stamps are difficult to locate and read.

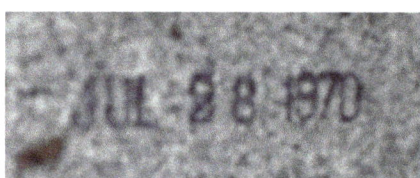
Figure 40 - Date Stamp on Granitone Interior (Kevin Oppendike)

The vast majority of Standard drums reported with date indicators have date stamps placed directly on the interior of Standard drum shells. The earliest and latest reports visually confirmed by the author are AUG 12 1968 and APR 13 1971. The practice of applying date stamps to the inside of the Standard shells appears to have been discontinued by about April 1971, which corresponds to the point that dates stop appearing stamped directly onto main line shells.

*2. Date Stamps on Paper Labels* In about mid-April 1971, Ludwig began to glue paper labels inside the shells of both its Standard and main line drums. The label included space for date and model number, which were presumably filled in during the assembly process. When the paper label was introduced, Ludwig continued with its practice of applying a date stamp in the same "JAN 01 1900" format that it used on the shells. The earliest confirmed report of a date stamp on a label on a Standard drum is APR 15 1971 and the latest is MAY 26 1971 on wood-shelled drums and JAN 3 1972 on metal-shelled drums.

---

[49] Interestingly, red ink stamps are generally not seen on main line drums after about 1965.

*3. Date Codes on Paper Labels*  Like on their main line brethren, in Ludwig began to apply a four or five digit code instead of the date stamp on labels on Standard drums.  This happened in about June 1971 for wood-shelled drums and January 1972 for metal-shelled drums.  Date Codes are more fully discussed in Part V.

Whether a Standard drum has a date stamp on its shell, a paper label with a date stamp or a paper label with a date code falls within general time frames.  A drum without a date indicator may appear at any time.  The rough timing of each style of date indicator is provided below.  This table may be helpful where date stamps are difficult to read or labels are damaged.

**Table 9**
**Date Ranges and Date Indication Styles on Standard Drums**
© Richard E. Gier, 2013, 2023

| Approximate Date Range | Style of Date Indication |
| --- | --- |
| Late 1968 to APR 1971 | Date Stamp on interior of shell |
| APR 1971 to MAY 1971 | Date Stamp on paper label - wood |
| APR 1971 to JAN 1972 | Date Stamp on paper label - metal |
| JUN 1971 to APR 1972 | Date Code on paper label - wood |
| JAN 1972 to APR 1972 | Date Code on paper label - metal |
| MAY 1972 to later | No date indicator |

## D. Serial Number/Date Stamp Relationship

Little is known about the specific process used to produce Standard drums.  For the purposes of this paper, it is assumed that similar procedures were used to produce both Ludwig main line and second line drums.  Standard shells were likely date stamped at the time of their creation, a date which might bear little relationship to when they were assembled into finished drums and received serialized badges.  With the main line drums, it has been suggested that the lack of control by either serial number or date introduced considerable variation to an orderly sequential and time-based use of serial numbers.  If similar procedures were used to produce Standards, then the issuance and use of serial numbers in strict sequential or date order is highly doubtful.  But, like with the main line drums, Standard drums exhibit a general tendency toward numerical order.  Also like the main line drums, many Standards do not possess date stamps at all.  Without specific knowledge of the process used to produce Standards, one must turn to the drums themselves to understand them.

Information from 215 drums which possess both date stamps and serial numbers is also shown below in Graph 7.  When graphed, the relationship between date and serial number is visually apparent.  A best fit line is calculated and added to the graph to provide a mid-point for date estimation purposes.

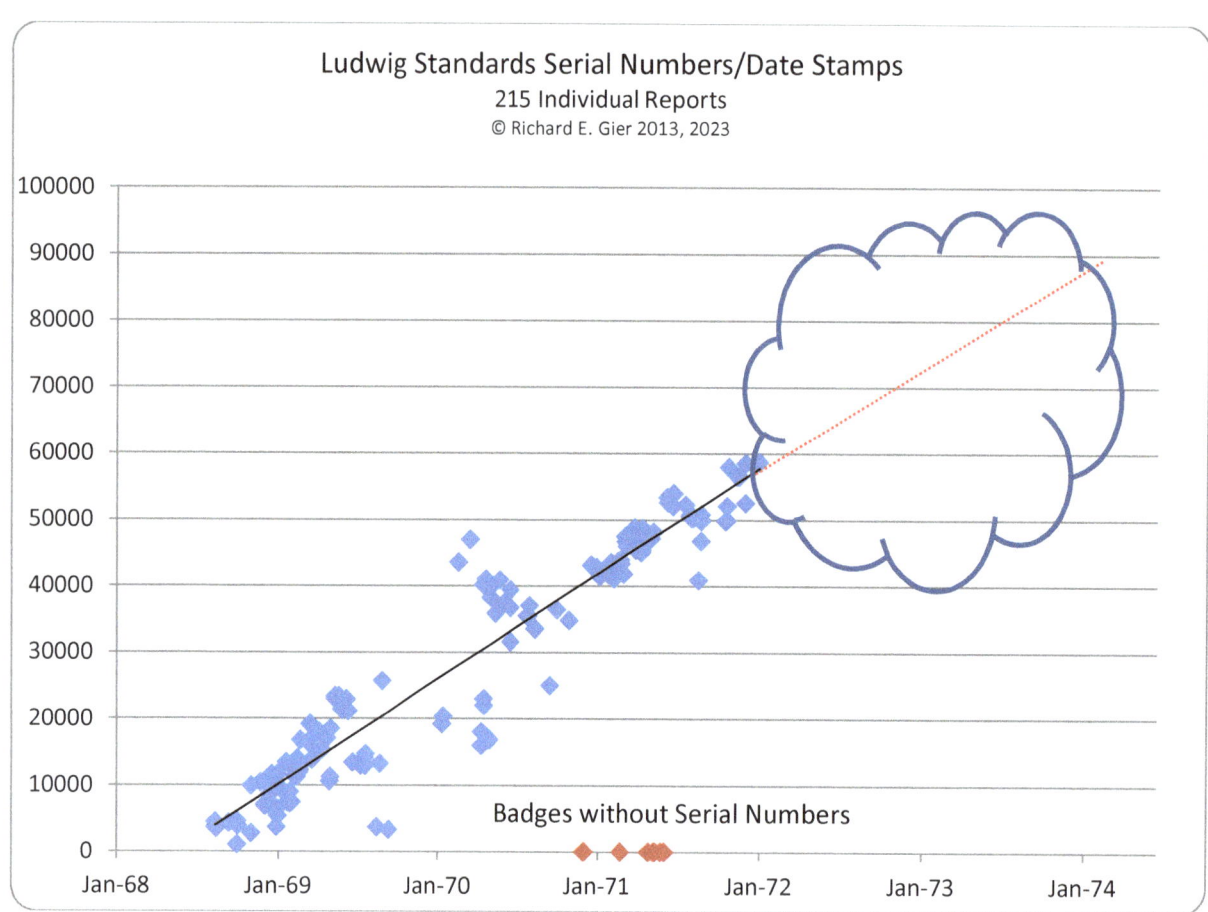

Graph 7 - Relationship Between Date Stamps and Serial Numbers for Standard Drums

Significant variation exists, so one cannot obtain a highly accurate date estimation by locating a point on the line shown on Graph 7. However, a rough estimate can be obtained by locating the serial number on the Y-axis, moving horizontally across to the line on the graph and then dropping down to the date on the X-axis. With more reports and a breakthrough regarding the proper interpretation of the Date Code, more refinements seem likely. Note that the line drawn on the graph represents a constant production rate. The rate may have varied by year or seasonally, but at this time, no specific information about the production rate of Standards is known.

These drums display a relatively consistent relationship between date stamps and serial numbers. Drums with lower serial numbers tend to have earlier dates than drums with higher serial numbers. Drum with serial numbers in the middle range have paper labels inside them. Drums with the highest serial numbers have no date indicators at all. Exceptions exist, but this general trend is fairly clear. Date stamps on shells appear on the lowest serial numbers through serial numbers in the 46000 range, with dates from late 1968 through March 1971. Labels with date stamps appear on drums in the 47000 – 59000 serial number range with date stamps from April 1971 through January 1972. Several drums with serial numbers between 49000 and 67000 have labels with Date Codes. The Date Code appears to have been used in the June 1971 to April 1972 time period. Additional exploration of Date Codes is described in Part V. Finally, there are many reports of drums with serial numbers above 67000 and below 96000, none of which is reported to possess any type of date indicator.

E. Interior Finish

The Granitone name was used for Ludwig's gray speckled Granitone interior finish when it was introduced in the 1968 Standards catalog. The same finish was called Lud-Cote when it was introduced on main line drums in about 1971. Many associate Standards with Granitone interior finish, but not all Standards have them. Wood shelled Standard drums initially received the familiar white Resa-Cote finish used on main line drums. It was not until about 1969 that the Granitone finish became the norm on wood shelled Standards. A few Standards have clear lacquer interiors. Examples of these three interior finishes are presented in Part III of this paper as Figures 11, 12 and 13. One model of Standards, the Single Six S-340, has nesting concert toms with wrap placed on the interiors of its shells to match the wrap on the exteriors.

Figure 41 –Wrap on Interior  (Kevin Oppendike)

Although not enough data is yet available to provide precise time estimates, tendencies are apparent regarding which interior finish is likely to be used. Examples of Standards with Resa-Cote interiors tend to be from drums with earlier dates and lower serial numbers. The Granitone interiors took over as dates became later and serial numbers rose. The transition point from Resa-Cote to Granitone does not seem to be sudden or definite, but occurred in the 1969 timeframe. The few reports of clear interior drums have serial numbers in the 37000-48000 range and date stamps from 1970 and 1971. Significant overlap is evident, with some apparently factory sets possessing drums with a mixture of different interior finishes.

**Table 10**
**Interior Finish Styles on Wood Shell Standard Drums**
© Richard E. Gier 2013, 2023

| Approximate Date Range | Interior Finish |
|---|---|
| 1968 to 1969 | Mainly Resa-Cote, some Granitone |
| 1970 to 1973 | Almost exclusively Granitone, some Clear |

As mentioned in Part III, the Resa-Cote interior finish appears on main line drums with date stamps until about April 1968. Clear interiors took over at that time. It was not until about 1971 that the Lud-Cote interior finish appeared in main line drums. Therefore, the Granitone/Lud-Cote finish was first introduced on Standards and did not come into use on main line B/O badge drums until a few years later. There appears to be little correlation between the interior finish on the main line drums and Standards. Whether this is intended as another way to differentiate the budget drums from the main drums is not clear, but Ludwig's concurrent use of two different names for the same finish provides a distinction between the main and second lines.

### F. Throw-Off / Butt Plate

Ludwig Standard snare drums are equipped with model P-83 throw-offs and model P-32 butt plates with the Ludwig logo typically in block lettering.[50] The corresponding versions of the P-83 throws and P-32 butts used on the main line drums had script lettering. However, Standard snares are reported with all combinations of script and block logos on their P-83 throws and P-32 butts. A detailed study of the logos on Standard throw-offs and butt plates is available for those seeking more information.[51]

In about 1969, on the main line drums, the script P-83 throw was replaced by a P-85 throw with a black face plate with block logo and 12 holes for snare wires. The same switch was not made with Standards, which retained their block logo P-83s. Some Standard snares today possess variations of the P-85 model throw-offs, including some later versions which are clearly post-factory replacements. It has not been determined if P-85 throws are ever factory installed in Standard snare drums.

Figure 42 - Detail of P-83 Throw with Block Logo    Figure 43 – Detail of P-83 Throw with Script Logo

### G. Hardware Variations

Like the number of throw-offs and butt plates with script logos, several reports have been documented of Standard badge drums which have hardware cataloged as being used on main line drums, such as classic or bowtie lug casings. It is popularly theorized that Ludwig periodically ran out of the correct Standard lug casings and substituted bowtie lug casings in order to meet production requirements. The explanation is usually presented along the lines of, "the hole spacing was the same, so such a switch would be relatively easy, and Ludwig did not care that the lug casings did not match." It is also likely that at least some of these drums have endured post-factory lug casing switches. Similar reports exist for substitutions of other types of hardware, i.e.: rail style tom mounts rather than the center post style mount which is shown in catalogs and appears on the vast majority of Standards. There is little doubt that such variations exist and many appear to be factory original. One can view these variations as charming nuances of Ludwig drums or as deviations which make the challenging puzzle of understanding Standard drums even more challenging. Not enough data has been gathered to identify any patterns for when such deviant drums were made or the actual reason that such alterations occurred.

---

[50] According to the trademark registration, the block logo was first used on March 28, 1969 and first used in commerce on June 1, 1969. The March 28, 1969 date corresponds to when P-85 throws are first observed on main line drums on about April 1, 1969 and predates the use of the block logo on B/O badges in late 1969. This same logo was used on Standard badges and catalogs beginning in 1968. It is possible that when Ludwig finally applied for trademark registration in 1979, the earlier use of the logo on second line Standards were overlooked.

[51] Richard E. Gier, "Logos on Ludwig Standard Snare Drum Throw-offs and Butt Ends," https://gretschdrumdatingguide.com/other-projects.html, October 31, 2021. Also available at https://www.notsomoderndrummer.com/not-so-modern-drummer/2021/10/29/logos-on-ludwig-standard-snare-drum-throw-offs-and-butt-ends

### H. Anti-Galvanic Plating Markings on Chrome Shells

Standards used the same Stamps as the main line chrome-plated drums during the same time frames. Initially, A-G Stamps appeared, but there are only two reports of them so far. One has serial number 29078 and the other has date stamp JAN 13 1970. Later Standards have "RELIABLE ANTI-GALVANIC" Stamps, with serial numbers ranging from 47319 to 87000 and date stamps ranging from DEC 3 1970 to DEC 3 1971. "RELIABLE ANTI-GALVANIC" stamps continued in use after date stamps were discontinued. They also appear on drums with Date Codes.

### I. Use This Guide with Caution

Plainly stated, this Dating Guide for Ludwig Standards does not provide precise date estimates. It is based upon a sample size comprising less than one-half of one percent of the Standard drums believed to be produced. Only about one-sixth of those had both serial numbers and useable date stamps. This guide is the most comprehensive published resource for Ludwig Standards produced in the 1968-1973 time frame. This claim can be made primarily because this guide is the only one available, not because it presents all of the answers. However, it is hoped that others who have an interest in these often overlooked drums will offer refinements to improve this guide.

## PART V – DECIPHERING THE DATE CODES

As described above, many Ludwig B/O Badge and Standard drums from 1971-72 have paper labels inside them. The paper labels have spaces for date and model number. Drums with labels with date stamps using the familiar "JAN 01 1900" type format are included in the Dating Guide presented in Parts II and IV above. Other drums with paper labels have four or five-digit numbers in the area for date, which are identified here as "Date Codes." The Date Code is usually stamped, although a few are handwritten. Twenty different Date Codes have been identified: 4272, 11472, 11717, 12717, 13727, 14717, 14720, 14727, 20717, 21720, 21727, 31720, 32372, 41727, 56717, 57717, 58717, 59717, 60717 and 61717. Two hundred ninety-three reports of Date Codes are recorded (245 main line, 48 Standards).[52] Some Date Codes appear only once, while ten appear more than ten times. The most frequently appearing Date Code, 56717, appears on forty-two different drums. The main line drums with Date Codes have BO1 badges with serial numbers ranging from about 824000 to about 938000. Standard drums with Date Codes have badges with serial numbers ranging from about 51000 to about 67000.

A separate article delves deeply into the short paper label era of Ludwig drums (about April 1971 through April 1972) and ferrets out when date stamps or Date Codes appeared on main line and Standard drums.[53] A summary of the key observations of that article is provided below:

1. Paper labels are first introduced in April 1971 with date stamps. They are used on wood shelled and metal shelled drums in both main line and Standard drums. Date Codes replaced date stamps on wood shelled drums in about June 1971.

2. It was not until the beginning of 1972 that the switch from date stamps to Date Codes occurs on metal shelled drums.

---

[52] Mike Machat contributed 26 reports of main line drums with Date Codes.
[53] Richard E. Gier, "Ludwig's Use of Paper Labels in 1971 / 1972 – Date Stamps and Date Codes," July 14, 2020 and Not So Modern Drummer - www.notsomoderndrummer.com/not-so-modern-drummer/2020/8/29/ludwigs-use-of-paper-labels-in-19711972-date-stamps-and-date-codes

3. From the beginning of 1972 through about March 1972, Date Codes are used on both wood and metal shelled drums.

4. Most interpretations of Date Codes offered by vintage drum enthusiasts are simply wrong. Most seem created to explain a single example of a drum with a single Date Code. For example, Date Code 4272 is often interpreted as representing April 2, 1972, while many of the Date Codes ending in the number seven are viewed as being from July. These explanations do not make sense when all 20 Date Codes used are considered. Many theories interpret the "71" or "72" present in every Date Code as indicators of the years 1971 and 1972, but fail to address the remaining digits.

5. Date Codes might not be date related at all, but could represent some other aspect of the manufacturing process like an employee number or some other production related number that was placed in that spot on the label (just to confuse vintage drum enthusiasts decades later).

6. Understanding the different treatment of wood and metal shelled drums with paper labels permits a reliable and supportable interpretation of part of the Date Code, namely that the "71" and "72" present within every Date Code are very likely indications of the years 1971 and 1972.

7. More investigation is needed to determine if additional information, like an indicator of month, can be shown to be imbedded in the Date Code.

## PART VI - BADGES WITHOUT SERIAL NUMBERS

It is not clear why Ludwig used badges without serial numbers or how many were used. A 2021 study looked at 332 vintage Ludwig drums that have badges without serial numbers.[54] Key observations from that study are included below.

Badges without serial numbers ("Blank Badges") have been recorded on K2, K3, K4, BO1, BO2, Standards and a silver parallelogram badge. Blank K2 badges are reported on shells which bear date stamps in September and October 1970. Contrary to popular belief, Blank K2 badges did not appear at the end of the Keystone badge era in late 1969 during the transition to B/O Badges.

> **MYTH - The first B/O badges lacked serial numbers and were used in 1969 when Ludwig discontinued the Keystone badge until Ludwig could order or produce B/O badges with serial numbers.**
> **TRUTH – Blank B/O badges generally appear on drums date stamped in 1970, a year after the transition from Keystone badges.**

Blank BO badges appear on a variety of different drum models while Trimmed BO badges are seen on metal snares with raised center beads - Acrolite, Suraphonic and Super Sensitive models. For these models, it is popularly explained that if the shell is drilled for a Keystone badge, the vent hole is located too close to the center bead to permit enough space for a full-sized Blue/Olive badge. Some BO1 and BO2 badges have had the lower portion where serial numbers would usually appear trimmed off ("Trimmed Badges"). It is not known if Trimmed BO badges ever had serial numbers. In addition, some later Trimmed BO badges appear on drums considered factory seconds or "B Stock" made in the

---

[54] Richard E. Gier, "Vintage Ludwig Badges without Serial Numbers - Prototypes, Limited Editions, Special Orders, Mistakes or Just Badges Lacking Serial Numbers?" https://gretschdrumdatingguide.com/other-projects.html and https://www.notsomoderndrummer.com/not-so-modern-drummer/2021/12/31/vintage-ludwig-badges-without-serial-numbers-prototypes-limited-editions-special-orders-mistakes-or-just-badges-lacking-serial-numbers, December 31, 2021.

1990s and 2000s. These should not be confused with the Trimmed BO badge of the 1970s era. Trimmed BO badges often are an indicator that the shell is brass rather than Ludaloy. Many brass-shelled drums also have a "B" stamped above the tone control knob, and lack the pitting and flaking which plagues chrome-plated Ludaloy shells. Caution should be exercised when considering Blank Badges because modern reproduction badges do not possess serial numbers and may be mistaken for vintage Blank Badges.

Figure 44 - Blank BO2 Badge (Mike Layton)    Figure 45 - Trimmed BO2 Badge (Mike Layton)

**MYTH – Vintage Ludwig drums with trimmed badges are factory seconds.**
**TRUTH – Badges on vintage Ludwig drums were trimmed to allow for the badge to be attached to vent holes which were located too low on the shell to accommodate the complete badge. Placing trimmed badges on factory seconds did not start until about 2000.**

A few Blank BO badges have had numbers etched into the area where the serial number would usually appear. Many of these "Etched Badges" appear to be factory original while some are clearly owner additions. One apparently factory etched badge has the etched serial number recorded on the original store receipt dated from 1970.[55] Silver badges, which are BO2 badges without the blue and olive paint, appear as Blank and Etched versions.

Figure 46 - Etched BO1 Badge (Tim Hornbeck)    Figure 47 - Etched BO2 Badge (Kevin Oppendike)

---

[55] Hand etched serial number 1006 and JUN 19 1970 date stamp on a drum reported by collector Tim Hornbeck.

## Table 11
### Blank, Trimmed and Etched Badges by Year (with Detail for 1970)
© Richard E. Gier 2021, 2023

| Dates | Blank K2 | Blank BO1 | Blank BO2 | Trimmed BO1 | Trimmed BO2 | Etched BO1 | Etched BO2 | Blank Silver | Etched Silver | Blank Standard |
|---|---|---|---|---|---|---|---|---|---|---|
| DEC 1969 | | | | 4 | | | | | | |
| JAN 1, 1970 – MAR 31, 1970 | | | | 12 | | | | | | |
| APR 1, 1970 - AUG 30, 1970 | | 20 | | 5 | | 2 | | | | |
| SEP 1, 1970 - OCT 10, 1970 | 17 | 59 | | | | 3 | | | | |
| OCT 10, 1970 - DEC 31, 1970 | | 1 | | 1 | | | | | | 4 |
| 1971 | | 34 | | 11 | | | | | | 11 |
| 1972 and later | | | 53 | | 16 | | 10 | 2 | 9 | |
| Unknown Date | 4 | 25 | | 17 | | | | | | 12 |
| Total | 21 | 139 | 53 | 50 | 16 | 5 | 10 | 2 | 9 | 27 |

Significant Time Periods:

December 1969 – March 1970 - Initial unnumbered badges were Trimmed BO1.

April 1970 - First documented Blank BO1 badges appear.

September 1 - October 9, 1970 - High concentration of Blank K2 and Blank BO1 badges.

1971 and later - Trimmed BO1 and BO2 badges are only on brass shelled drums.

## Acknowledgements:

Several drum collector/historians assisted in this effort. Steve Black, Mike Layton and Mike Machat generously shared serial number and date stamp information and their vintage drum knowledge. Rob Cook shared the information used to create his original dating guide. Paolo Sburlati, Kevin Oppendike and Tim Hornbeck shared their thoughts as well. Mike Bernazzani provided proofreading assistance. The assistance of all these individuals is greatly appreciated. Kevin Oppendike (Figures 7, 8, 37, 40, 41 & 47); Mike Layton (Figures 9, 10, 44 & 45); Mike Machat (Figure 27); Supersonic Music, Topeka, Kansas (Figures 32 & 35); Matt Jansen, Midwest Drum, Wichita, Kansas (Figure 33); Richard Blanchard, Mrfathead Drums, Arnold, Maryland (Figure 34) and Tim Hornbeck (Figure 46) provided pictures which are used with their permission. The owners reserve their ownership rights in these pictures. Copyright in the entire publication and author's pictures (all pictures without separate photo credit) is reserved by the author.

## COPYRIGHT INFRINGEMENT:

The prior edition of this book suffered frequent infringement, so this note is added. The preparation of this book involved thousands of hours of hard work. The author retains all rights, including the right to reproduce, distribute, sell and display this work and to create derivative works based upon this work. You cannot scan or take a picture of an important table or graph and post it on an internet site - it violates the author's intellectual property rights. This is not excused by fair use exceptions to US Trademark law. It also does not matter that you did not make any money from this act – what matters is the impact on potential sales of the publication. Please honor my creative rights.

**Please report your drums so they can be considered in future editions of this guide and see the Ludwig section of www.GretschDrumDatingGuide.com for updates.**

Serial Number: _____

Badge Style:  K1  K2  BO1  BO2  BO3  BO4  K3  K4  Standard  Other_____

Dimensions (inches):  Depth _____ x Diameter _____

Date Stamp?  Y / N

Date Stamp Color:  Black   Red

Paper Label?  Y / N

Date Code: _____

Tone Control Style:   Baseball Bat   Small Round Knob   Large Round Knob   None

Tone Control Mount Screws:  One Below Knob   One Above Knob   Three Below Knob   Three Above Knob

Tone Control location:    Above the Badge     Different Panel from Badge

Felt Type:   Red Rectangle   White Rectangle   Gray Round   Black Round

Interior Finish:  Resa-Cote (White)   Clear Varnish   Granitone/Lud-Cote   Unfinished

Exterior Wrap or Finish: _____

Number of heads:    One (Concert Tom)   Two

Number of lugs per head: _____

Throwoff:  P83  P84  P85 Black 12  P85 Black 2  P87  Classic  SuperSensitive  Other _____

Set Configuration (depth x dia):   \_\_x\_\_ ,  \_\_x\_\_ ,  \_\_x\_\_ ,  \_\_x\_\_ ,  \_\_x\_\_ ,  \_\_x\_\_ ,  \_\_x\_\_

Model:  Pioneer  JazzFestival  Acrolite  Supraphonic  Supersensitve  Clubdate  Classic
          Standard  Vistalite  Other _____  Model Number (if indicated) _____

Original Purchase Date (if known): _____

Other information: _____
_____
_____

Email your reports to:   Rick@GretschDrumDatingGuide.com

# REBEATS PUBLICATIONS

THE GRETSCH DRUM BOOK
by Rob Cook
with John Sheridan
Business history, dating guide

THE SLINGERLAND BOOK
by Rob Cook
Business history, dating guide

THE ROGERS BOOK
by Rob Cook
Business history, dating guide

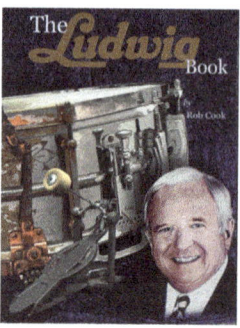
THE LUDWIG BOOK
by Rob Cook
Business history, dating guide

THE MAKING OF A DRUM COMPANY
The autobiography of Wm. F. Ludwig II,

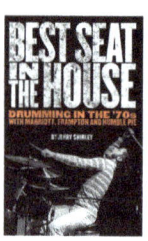
BEST SEAT IN THE HOUSE
Jerry Shirley memoir

Franks For The Memories

LEEDY DRUM TOPICS

THE LEEDY WAY
Biography of George Way,
History of Leedy, Camco, Conn, L&S

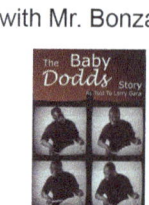
HAL BLAINE & THE WRECKING CREW
Memoir of Hal Blaine with Mr. Bonzai

Lucky Drummer
Ed Shaughnessy memoir

GENE KRUPA, HIS LIFE AND TIMES
biography of Gene Krupa,

Gretsch 1941 Catalog Reprint

THE BABY DODDS STORY

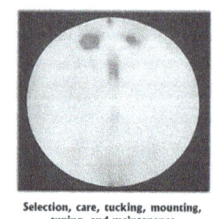
THE REBEATS CALFSKIN HEAD BOOK

George Way mini-bio, vendor directory

Gretsch Serial Number Dating Guide
by Rick Gier

Ludwig Serial Number Dating Guide
by Rick Gier

MY LIFE IN PERCUSSION
Five Decades In The Music Products Industry
Karl Dustman memoir

P.O. Box 6, Alma, Michigan 48801
989 463 4757
www.Rebeats.com   rob@rebeats.com

www.ingramcontent.com/pod-product-compliance
Ingram Content Group UK Ltd.
Pitfield, Milton Keynes, MK11 3LW, UK
UKHW062045180426
11947UKWH00030B/2060